NO EASY WALK TO FREEDOM

NELSON MANDELA

NO EASY WALK TO FREEDOM

Heinemann · Mandarin

A Mandarin Paperback

NO EASY WALK TO FREEDOM

First published by Heinemann Educational Books 1965
First published in African Writer's Series as AWS 123 in 1973
Reprinted (twelve times)
This edition published 1990
by Mandarin Paperbacks
Michelin House, 81 Fulham Road, London SW3 6RB

Mandarin is an imprint of the Octopus Publishing Group

Copyright © Nelson Mandela 1965

A CIP catalogue record for this title
is available from the British Library

ISBN 0 7493 0504 5

Printed in Great Britain
by Cox & Wyman Ltd, Reading

CONTENTS

INTRODUCTION

MANDELA AND TAMBO said the brass plate on our office door. We practised as attorneys-at-law in Johannesburg in a shabby building across the street from the Magistrates' Court. Chancellor House in Fox Street was one of the few buildings in which African tenants could hire offices: it was owned by Indians. This was before the axe of the Group Areas Act fell to declare the area 'White' and landlords were themselves prosecuted if they did not evict the Africans. MANDELA AND TAMBO was written huge across the frosted window panes on the second floor, and the letters stood out like a challenge. To White South Africa it was bad enough that two men with black skins should practise as lawyers, but it was indescribably worse that the letters also spelled out our political partnership.

Nelson and I were both born in the Transkei, he one year after me. We were students together at Fort Hare University College. With others we had founded the African National Congress Youth League. We went together into the Defiance Campaign of 1952, into general strikes against the Government, and sat in the same Treason Trial dock.

For years we worked side by side in the offices near the courts. To reach our desks each morning Nelson and I ran the gauntlet of patient queues of people overflowing from the chairs in the waiting-room into the corridors. South Africa has the dubious reputation of boasting one of the highest prison populations in the world. Jails are jam-packed with Africans imprisoned for serious offences—and crimes of violence are ever on the increase in apartheid society—but also for petty infringements of statutory law that no really civilized society would punish with imprisonment. To be unemployed is a crime because no African can for long evade arrest if his passbook does not carry the stamp of authorized and approved employment. To be landless can be a crime, and weekly we interviewed the delegations of grizzled, weather-worn peasants from the countryside who came to tell us how many generations their families had worked a little piece of land from which they were now being ejected. To brew African beer, to drink it or to use the proceeds to supplement the meagre family income is a crime, and women who do so face heavy fines and jail terms. To cheek a White man can be a crime. To live in the 'wrong' area—an area declared White or Indian or Coloured—can be a crime for Africans. South African apartheid laws turn innumerable innocent people into 'criminals'. Apartheid stirs hatred and frustration among people. Young people who should be in school or learning a trade roam the streets, join gangs and wreak their revenge on the society that confronts them with only the dead-end alley of crime or poverty. Our buff office files carried thousands of these stories and if, when we started our law partnership, we had not been rebels against South African apartheid, our experiences in our offices would have remedied the deficiency. We had risen to professional status in our community, but every case in court, every visit to the prisons to interview clients, reminded us of the humiliation and suffering burning in tour people.

Nelson, one of the royal family of the Transkei, was groomed from childhood for respectability, status, and sheltered living. Born near Umtata in 1918, he was the eldest son of a Tembu chief. His father died when he was twelve and his upbringing and education were taken over by the Paramount Chief. Nelson, Sabata, Paramount Chief of the Tembu and opponent of the Government, and Kaizer Matanzima, Chief Minister of the Transkei and arch-collaborator with the Nationalist Government, were educated together. At the age of sixteen, Nelson went to Fort Hare and there we first met: in the thick of a student strike.

After Fort Hare we parted company. I went on to teach mathematics at St Peter's School in Johannesburg. From this school, killed by the Government in later years because it refused to bow its head to Government-dictated principles of a special education for 'inferior' Africans (Bantu education), graduated successive series of young men drawn inexorably into the African National Congress because it was the head of our patriotic, national movement for our rights.

Nelson ran away from the Transkei to escape a tribal marriage his cousins and uncles were trying to arrange for him. In Johannesburg he had his first encounter with the lot of the urban African in a teeming African township: overcrowding, incessant raids for passes, arrests, poverty, the pin-pricks and frustrations of White rule. Walter Sisulu, secretary-general of the African National Congress in a vital period, befriended and advised and urged him to study law. Mandela studied by correspondence to gain an arts degree, enrolled for a law degree at the University of the Witwatersrand and was later articled to a firm of White attorneys. We met again in 1944 in the ranks of the African National Congress Youth League.

As a man Nelson is passionate, emotional, sensitive, quickly stung to bitterness and retaliation by insult and patronage. He has a natural air of authority. He cannot help magnetizing a crowd: he is commanding with a tall, handsome bearing; trusts and is trusted by the youth, for their impatience reflects his own; appealing to the women. He is dedicated and fearless. He is the born mass leader.

But early on he came to understand that State repression was too savage to permit mass meetings and demonstrations through which the people could ventilate their grievances and hope for redress. It was of limited usefulness to head great rallies. The Government did not listen and soon enough the tear gas and the muzzles of the guns were turned against the people. The justice of our cries went unrecognized. The popularity of leaders like Mandela was an invitation to counter-attack by the Government. Mandela was banned from speaking, from attending gatherings, from leaving Johannesburg, from belonging to any organization. Speeches, demonstrations, peaceful protests, political organizing, became illegal.

Of all that group of young men, Mandela and his close friend and co-leader Walter Sisulu were perhaps the fastest to get to grips with the harsh realities of the African struggle against the most powerful adversary in Africa: a highly industrialized, well-armed State manned by a fanatical group of White men determined to defend their privilege and their prejudice, and aided by the complicity of American, British, West German, and Japanese investment in the most profitable system of oppression on the continent. Nelson was a key figure in thinking, planning, and devising new tactics.

We had to forge an alliance of strength based not on colour but on commitment to the total abolition of apartheid and oppression; we would seek allies, of whatever colour, as long as they were totally agreed on our liberation aims. The African people, by nature of their numbers, their militancy, and the grimness of their oppression, would be the spearhead of the struggle. We had to organize the people, in town and countryside, as an instrument for struggle. Mandela drafted the M plan, a simple commonsense plan for organization on a street basis so that Congress volunteers would be in daily touch with the people, alert to their needs and able to mobilize them. He no longer appeared on the public platform, and few platforms were allowed us as the years went by, but he was ever among the people, guiding his lieutenants to organize them. During the Treason Trial these efforts at organization were put on trial. Mandela went from prison cell to dock and then to witness-box when the accused conducted their defence and he and his co-accused expounded the policy of Congress in court. The men in the dock were acquitted but the trial marked the end of that epoch and the opening of a new one.

By 1960 virtually every African leader was muzzled and restricted by Government decree. There was no right to organize. In March 1960 there were the anti-pass protests called by the breakaway Pan-Africanist Congress, and the peaceful gathering at Sharpeville was machine-gunned. The ANC called for a national protest strike. The country answered that call. The ANC was declared illegal, together with the Pan-Africanist Congress. In a five-month-long state of emergency virtually every known Congressman was imprisoned, but during the Emergency and even more so immediately afterwards the ANC put itself on an underground footing. Now Mandela's M plan came into its own. Ever at the centre, pulling the strings together, inspiring the activities that, if apprehended, could mean long stretches in prison for ANC activists, was Nelson.

In May 1961 South Africa was to be declared a Nationalist Republic. There was a White referendum, but no African was consulted. The African people decided there were ways of making their opposition felt. A general strike would be the answer. The strike was called in the name of Nelson Mandela. He left his home, our office, his wife and children, to live the life of a political outlaw. Here began the legend of the Black Pimpernel. He lived in hiding, meeting only his closest political associates, travelling round the country in disguise, popping up here to lead and advise, disappearing again when the hunt got too hot.

The strike was smashed by an unprecedented police and army mobilization. If peaceful protests like these were to be put down by force then the people would be forced to use other methods of struggle, was the inevitable conclusion. The ANC was no longer merely a national patriotic front, it was an underground resistance struggle. Acts of sabotage shook the country from the second half of 1961. Umkonto we Sizwe (the Spear of the Nation) had been formed and was at work.

I had left South Africa early in 1960, sent out by the ANC to open our offices abroad. Mandela was then in prison during the state of emergency proclaimed after Sharpeville. I saw him again, astonishingly, in 1961 and 1962 when he left his hiding places somewhere in South Africa, was smuggled across the border, and turned up at the Addis Ababa conference of the Pan-African Freedom Movement of East and Central Africa to expound before the delegates the policy for struggle of our organization and our people.

In South Africa the freedom fight has grown grim and relentless. Mandela went home to survive a perilous existence underground for seventeen months until he was betrayed by an informer and sentenced to five years' imprisonment for his leadership of the 1961 strike and for leaving the country illegally. From his cell he was taken to the dock in the Rivonia trial to face trial with eight others, among them Walter Sisulu. The charge was sabotage and conspiracy to overthrow the Government by force. The world watched that trial and knows the verdict of guilty and the sentence of life imprisonment. Nelson Mandela is on Robben Island today. His inspiration lives on in the heart of every African patriot. He is the symbol of the self-sacrificing leadership our struggle has thrown up and our people need. He is unrelenting, yet capable of flexibility and delicate judgement. He is an outstanding individual, but he knows that he derives his strength from the great masses of people who make up the freedom struggle in our country.

I am convinced that the world-wide protests during the Rivonia trial saved Mandela and his fellow-accused from a death sentence. But in South Africa a life sentence means imprisonment until death—or until the defeat of the Government which holds these men prisoner. The sentences they serve are a searing reminder that such men must not be wasted behind bars; that no solution to South Africa's conflict can be found while the people are deprived of such leadership; that Mandela is imprisoned not for his personal defiance of apartheid law but because he asserted the claims of a whole people living and dying under the most brutal system of race rule the world knows.

OLIVER TAMBO

Dar-es-Salaam
December 1964

EDITORIAL NOTE

THE material here published—eleven articles, one conference speech made while abroad, and evidence and addresses from three trials—spans a period of ten years, from 1953 to 1963, when Mandela had to use the pen instead of the microphone (except the official one, in court) to address his people. Many speeches made by him in the years before he was banned from speaking are recorded in South African police archives, but are unavailable for a book like this.

The articles are reproduced almost exactly as they were written, with light editing only here and there to omit repetition or local references that would have meaning only for South Africans—who, incidentally, may not read this book, because it is an offence in South Africa to circulate the words of a 'banned' person. In the court addresses passages relating to the technical evidence in the testimony of certain state witnesses have been deleted.

Some of the articles have been taken out of their strict time sequence to permit a clearer arrangement of the material against the background of events in South Africa, which rose to steady climax until the fateful final trial.

The commentaries prefacing each piece serve briefly to trace the events to which Mandela responded with ever-growing courage.

R.F.

STREAMS OF
AFRICAN NATIONALISM

I

THE union of South Africa's four provinces in 1910 was a union of White privilege and power for African subjection. Africans had no vote, no freedom of movement or civic rights, and they were being steadily deprived of their land. Africans (called 'kaffirs') had to take off their hats when passing White men and they were pushed off the pavements into the gutter if they did not know their place.

The last tribal military rising had been defeated in 1904. Tribal organization had begun to give way to national organization. Men were no longer Xhosa, Pondo or Tembu, Zulu, Bechuana, Shangaan or Basuto. They were Africans. But early political organization was hesitant and scattered until in 1912 at Bloemfontein the South African Native National Congress was formed, later to be renamed the African National Congress of today. The founders of this body were African lawyers, clerks, clergymen, journalists and teachers, a sprinkling of educated urban middle-class men; and august tribal chiefs and traditional peasant leaders from the rural areas.

The Congress modelled itself in structure on the American Congress and the House of Lords. It appointed a sergeant-at-arms who carried the mace, and a Speaker, and it elevated the Chiefs to an Upper House. It appealed to the British Government, its mentor in parliamentary procedures, to intervene on the side of the African people, because impassioned pleas to the South African Government to alleviate the plight of the African people were being met only with the piling on of the burden of oppression.

The Congress took deputations to Britain, to the Pan-African Congress of 1919, even to Versailles. There was, of course, no intervention.

At home Congress worked for the redress of its grievances by 'constitutional' methods, by arguing for the removal of the colour-bar in Parliament, in education, in industry, in the administration. White government had for decades talked of the unfitness of uneducated Africans to govern. Africans lived in hope of educating the White electorate, enlisting their sympathy and gradually persuading them to make room for industrious and thrifty Africans. In many hearts this must have been a futile hope as petitions, deputations, and pleas made no dent in the wall of White policy.

It took the unrest during and after the 1914–18 war to open flood-gates of protest. Women of the Orange Free State rose against passes on the eve of the war. The first African strike, of sanitary workers in Johannesburg, broke in 1919. The same year saw the first of many passive resistance protest campaigns against passes. Forty thousand African miners struck for higher wages. Again in the 1920s African women rose against passes.

Congress changed its name in 1925 to the S.A. African National Congress, and adopted a flag: black for the African people, green for the land, gold for the riches underground.

In the 'twenties and 'thirties a general union, the Industrial and Commercial Workers Union (ICU), swept the country, snatching the initiative of organizing the Africans being absorbed in town and industry. Annual conferences of Congress were large and representative, but the force of its leadership was blunted by the outlook that Africans might yet win White and official sympathy by the exercise of modera-tion and patience. Africans stung to angry political response by their conditions tended to gather under other banners: the ICU, trade unions, the Communist Party.

The leadership of the moderate men failed the crucial tests of 1935–6 when a final seal was placed on the Government policy of segregation. At the All-African Convention summoned at Bloemfontein, where Congress and other African leaders gathered, a minority call for action was defeated.

A great army of the urban dispossessed was growing. The migrant labourer worked in mine and farm for most of the year and then returned to the segregated Reserves; he lived long enough in giant compounds with labour drawn from all southern Africa to learn first principles of organization and unity. Some strikes were broken by police violence; others won victories. The Indian people launched a passive resistance struggle in 1939 and another in 1946 and their example did not go unnoticed.

The pressures of the 'forties and a new war brought change. Congress gave itself a new constitution, a more democratic one, which abolished the House of Chiefs; and a new president reorganized the branches.

And a Youth League was founded. A new generation turned to political action. Some were self-educated workers like Walter Sisulu and Anton Lembede. Some, like Nelson Mandela, were sons of chiefs. The young men passed through mission schools, studied on bursaries, read textbooks but also newspapers, and became infected by discontent with an outspoken and vigorous nationalism. The Youth League openly attacked past policies of Congress, the leadership of the 'moderates', vacillation, and compromise. The militant ideas of the Youth Leaguers were a forerunner to the rise of African nationalism in West and East Africa.

These two streams, the dynamism of the youth and the militancy of a growing African working-class movement, converged on Congress and changed it. In 1945 the ANC adopted 'African claims'. The cry was sharply for one man one vote, equal justice in the courts, freedom of land ownership, the repeal of the pass laws.

The great African mine strike of 1946 reverberated in the debating chambers of the Native Representative Council (a Government advisory council) and the tactic of boycott was adopted by chiefs, traders, intellectuals—the 'moderates'.

Now Congress annual conferences began to pound out schemes for mass struggles. This culminated in the adoption, under heavy Youth League pressure, of the 1949 Programme of Action, which advocated the use of boycott, strikes, non-cooperation, and civil disobedience, to achieve national freedom.

The Nationalist Government had come to power one year before the adoption of the Programme of Action. Segregation had been bitter enough; apartheid was vitriol. Differences between Whites and Africans were permanent and not man-made, the secretary of the then Prime Minister, Dr D. F. Malan, wrote to Walter Sisulu in 1952. Africans could hope for no relief now or at any time in the future.

The Suppression of Communism Act was passed. The stated objective of the measure was the outlawing of the Communist Party and communism but all except the politically artless read for 'Communist Party' all African opposition . . . and after that all militant anti-Nationalist opposition. The ANC called for strikes against the law.

Over the years the exclusive nationalism of the early Youth Leaguers was transformed through the experience of joint campaigning of Africans, Indians, Coloureds, and some Whites. In the Treason Trial, Mandela was later to expound the aims of African nationalism:

'There are two streams of African nationalism. One centres round Marcus Garvey's slogan "Africa for the Africans". It is based on the "quit Africa" slogan and on the cry "Hurl the White man into the sea". This brand of African nationalism is extreme and ultra-revolutionary. There is another stream of African nationalism, Africanism, which the Congress Youth League professes. We of the Youth League take account of the concrete situation in South Africa and realize that the different racial groups have come to stay, but we insist that a condition for inter-racial peace and progress is the abandonment of White domination and such a change in the basic structure of South African society that those relations which breed exploitation and human misery will disappear. Therefore our goal is the winning of national freedom for the African people and the inauguration of a peoples' free society where racial oppression and persecution will be outlawed.'

In the 1952 Campaign of Defiance of Unjust Laws, 8,500 volunteers went to prison for deliberate acts of civil disobedience against six selected apartheid laws. Nelson Mandela was national volunteer-in-chief of the campaign, and he was responsible for the selection of volunteers and for laying down their code of discipline.

The ANC grew enormously in influence. For some previous weeks it held in its hands the political initiative in the country. Unarmed, undisciplined, Africans—side by side with Indians, Coloureds, and a sprinkling of White volunteers—were defying the law. Their demands were articulate and non-racialist. They had a blueprint for a democratic new society and they were steeling their political organization for a confrontation with the Government.

The Government cracked down. Its reprisals included blanket powers to impose unlimited periods of martial law, and savage sentences including lashes for civil disobedience. The definition of civil disobedience was any infringement of any law by way of protest. Passive resistance as a form of struggle was declared illegal.

The ANC entered the next stage of the battle with a greatly invigorated following, a tried leadership and a sharply defined policy of struggle.

For his part as national volunteer-in-chief of the Defiance Campaign Mandela had been served Government orders which confined him to Johannesburg and banned him from attending or addressing gatherings. He was elected president of the Transvaal ANC, but was forbidden to address his following. So Mandela wrote out his presidential address for the 1953 annual conference and, when the proceedings were declared open, Robert Resha rose on the platform and read the speech in the name of Mandela.

NO EASY WALK TO FREEDOM

SINCE 1912 and year after year thereafter, in their homes, in provincial and national gatherings, on trains and buses, in the factories and on the farms, in cities, villages, shanty-towns, schools and prisons, the African people have discussed the shameful misdeeds of those who rule the country.

Year after year they have raised their voices to condemn the grinding poverty of the people, the low wages, the acute shortage of land, the inhuman exploitation, and the whole policy of White domination. But instead of more freedom, repression began to grow in volume and intensity and it seemed that all their sacrifices would end in smoke and dust.

Today the whole country knows that their labours were not in vain, for a new spirit and new ideas have gripped our people. Today the people speak the language of action: there is a mighty awakening among the men and women of our country.

The year 1952 stands out as the year of this upsurge of national consciousness. In June of that year African National Congress and the South African Indian Congress, bearing in mind their responsibility as the representatives of the downtrodden and oppressed people of South Africa, took the plunge and launched the campaign for the Defiance of Unjust Laws. Starting in Port Elizabeth in the early hours of 26 June and with only thirty-three defiers in action, and then in Johannesburg in the afternoon of the same day with 106 defiers, it spread throughout the country like wildfire. Factory and office-workers, doctors, lawyers, teachers, students, and the clergy; Africans, Coloureds, Indians, and Europeans, old and young, all rallied to the national call and defied the pass laws and the curfew and the railway apartheid regulations. By the end of the year, 8,500 people of all races had defied. The Campaign called for immediate and heavy sacrifices. Workers lost their jobs, chiefs and teachers were expelled from the service, doctors, lawyers, and businessmen gave up their practices and businesses and elected to go to jail. Defiance was a step of great political significance. It released stronger social forces which affected thousands of our countrymen.

It was an effective way of getting the masses to function politically; a powerful method of voicing our indignation against the reactionary policies of the Government. It was one of the best ways of exerting pressure on the Government and extremely dangerous to the stability and security of the State. It inspired and aroused our people from a conquered and servile community of 'yes-men' to a militant and uncompromising band of comrades-in-arms.

The entire country was transformed into battle zones where the forces of liberation were locked in immortal conflict against those of reaction and evil. Our flag flew in every battlefield, and thousands of our countrymen rallied around it.

We held the initiative and the forces of freedom were advancing on all fronts. It was against this background and at the height of this campaign that we held our last annual provincial conference in Pretoria in October last year. In a way that conference was a welcome reception for those who had returned from the battle-fields and a farewell to those who were still going into action. The spirit of defiance and action dominated the entire conference.

Today we meet under totally different conditions. By the end of July last year the campaign had reached a stage where it had to be suppressed by the Government or it would impose its own policies on the country. The Government launched its reactionary offensive, and struck at us.

Between July last year and August this year, forty-seven leading members from both Congresses in Johannesburg, Port Elizabeth, and Kimberley were arrested, tried, and convicted for launching the Defiance Campaign and given suspended sentences ranging from three months to two years, on condition that they did not again participate in the defiance of the unjust laws.

A proclamation was passed which prohibited meetings of more than ten Africans and made it an offence for any person to call upon an African to defy. Contravention of this proclamation carried a penalty of three years or a fine of £300.

The Government passed the so-called Public Safety Act which empowered it to declare a state of emergency and to create conditions which permit of the most ruthless and pitiless methods of suppressing our movement. Almost simultaneously, the Criminal Law Amendment Act was passed, which provided heavy penalties for those convicted of defiance offences. This

Act also made provision for the whipping of defiers, including women.

The Government also made extensive use of the Suppression of Communism Act. Last year, the Government ordered Moses Kotane, Yusuf Dadoo, J. B. Marks, David Bopape, and Johnson Ngwevela to resign from the Congresses and many other organizations and prohibited them from attending political gatherings. In consequence of these bans, Moses Kotane, J. B. Marks, and David Bopape did not attend our last provincial conference.

In December the secretary-general, Mr W. M. Sisulu, and I were banned from attending gatherings and confined to Johannesburg for six months. Early this year, the president-general, Chief Lutuli, while in the midst of a national tour which he was executing with remarkable energy and devotion, was prohibited from attending public gatherings and from visiting Durban, Johannesburg, Cape Town, Port Elizabeth, and many other centres.

A few days before the president-general was banned, the president of the South African Indian Congress, Dr G. M. Naicker, had been served with similar notice. Many active workers both from the African and Indian Congresses and from trade union organizations were also banned. The Congresses realized that these measures created a new situation which did not prevail when the campaign was launched in June 1952. The tide of defiance was bound to recede and we were forced to pause and to take stock of the new situation. We had to analyse the dangers that faced us, formulate plans to overcome them and evolve new plans of political struggle. A political movement must keep in touch with reality and the prevailing conditions.

Long speeches, the shaking of fists, the banging of tables, and strongly worded resolutions out of touch with conditions do not bring about mass action, and can do a great deal of harm to the organization and the struggles we serve. We understood that the masses had to be made ready for the new forms of political struggle. We had to recuperate our strength and muster our forces for another and more powerful offensive against the enemy. To have gone ahead blindly as if nothing had happened, would have been suicidal and stupid. The conditions under which we meet today are, therefore, vastly different. The Defiance Campaign, together with its thrills and adventures, has receded. The old methods of bringing about mass action through public mass meetings, press statements, and leaflets calling upon the people to go into action have become extremely dangerous and difficult to use effectively. The authorities will not easily permit a meeting called under the auspices of the ANC; few newspapers will publish statements openly criticizing the policies of the Government, and there is hardly a single printing press which will agree to print leaflets calling upon workers to embark upon industrial action, for fear of prosecution under the Suppression of Communism Act and similar measures.

These developments require the evolution of new forms of political struggle which will make it possible for us to strive for action on a higher level than the Defiance Campaign. The Government, alarmed by the indomitable upsurge of national consciousness, is doing everything in its power to crush our movement by removing the genuine representatives of the people from the organization. According to a statement made by Swart* in Parliament on 18 September 1953, there are thirty-three trade union officials and eighty-nine other people who have been served with notices in terms of the Suppression of Communism Act. This does not include that formidable array of freedom fighters who have been named and black-listed under the Suppression of Communism Act and those who have been banned under the Riotous Assemblies Act.

Meanwhile, the living conditions of the people, already extremely difficult, are steadily worsening and becoming unbearable. The purchasing power of the people is progressively declining and the cost of living is rocketing. Bread is now dearer than it was two months ago. The cost of milk, meat, and vegetables is beyond the pockets of the average family and many of our people cannot afford them. The people are too poor to have enough food to feed their families and children. They cannot afford sufficient clothing, housing, and medical care. They are denied the right to security and where allowances are paid in the event of unemployment, sickness, disability, and old age they are far too low for survival.

Because of lack of proper medical amenities our people are ravaged by such dreaded diseases as tuberculosis, venereal disease, pellagra; the infant mortality rate is very high. The

* Then South Africa's Minister of Justice—*Ed.*

recent State budget made provision for the increase of cost-of-living allowances for Europeans but not a word was said about the poorest and most hard-hit sections of the population, the African people.

The insane policies of the Government which have brought about an explosive situation in the country have scared foreign capital away from South Africa and the financial crisis through which the country is now passing is forcing many industrial and business concerns to close down, to retrench their staffs. Unemployment is growing every day. The farm labourers are in a particularly dire plight. You will perhaps recall the investigations and exposures of the semi-slave conditions on the Bethal farms made in 1948 by the Reverend Michael Scott and a *Guardian* correspondent; by *Drum* last year and *Advance* this year. You will recall how human beings, wearing only sacks with holes for their head and arms, never given enough food to eat, sleep on cement floors on cold nights with only their sacks to cover their shivering bodies. You will remember how they are woken as early as 4 a.m. and taken to work in the fields with their 'indunas' sjambokking those who try to straighten their backs, who feel weak or drop down because of hunger or sheer exhaustion. You will recall the story of human beings toiling pathetically from the early hours of the morning till sunset, fed only on mealie meal served on filthy sacks spread on the ground, and eating with their dirty hands. People falling ill are not given medical attention. You will also recall the revolting story of a farmer convicted for tying a labourer by his feet from a tree, having him flogged to death and pouring boiling water into his mouth when he cried for water. These things which have long vanished from many parts of the world still flourish in South Africa today. None will deny that they constitute a serious challenge to Congress, and we are duty bound to find an effective remedy to these obnoxious practices.

The Government has introduced in Parliament the Native Labour (Settlement of Disputes) Bill, and the Bantu Education Bill. Speaking of the Labour Bill, the Minister of Labour, Ben Schoeman, openly stated that an aim of this wicked measure is to allow African trade unions to die. By forbidding strikes and lock-outs, it deprives Africans of the one weapon workers have to improve their position. The aim of the measure is to destroy the present African trade unions which are controlled by the workers themselves and which fight for the improvement of their working conditions, in return for a Central Native Labour Board controlled by the Government and which will be used to frustrate the legitimate aspirations of the African worker.

The Minister of Native Affairs, Dr Verwoerd, has been brutally clear in explaining the objects of the Bantu Education Bill. According to him the aim of this law is to teach our children that Africans are inferior to Europeans. African education is to be taken out of the hands of people who taught equality between black and white. When this Bill becomes law it will not be the parents but the Department of Native Affairs which will decide whether an African child should receive higher or other education. It might well be that the children of those who criticize the Government and who fight its policies will be taught how to drill rocks in the mines and how to plough potatoes on the farms at Bethal. Higher education might well be the privilege of those children whose families have a tradition of collaboration with the ruling settlers. The attitude of the Congress to these Bills is very clear and unequivocal. Congress totally rejects both Bills without reservation. To accept measures of this nature, even in a qualified manner, will be a betrayal of the toiling masses. At a time when every genuine Congressite should fight unreservedly for the recognition of African trade unions and the realization of the principle that everyone has the right to form and to join trade unions for protecting his interests, we declare our firm belief in the principles enunciated in the Universal Declaration of Human Rights that everyone has the right to education; that education should be directed to the full development of the human personality, and to the strengthening of respect for human rights and fundamental freedoms. It shall promote understanding, tolerance, and friendship among the nations, racial or religious groups and shall further the activities of the United Nations for the maintenance of peace. The parents shall have the right to choose the kind of education that should be given to their children.

The cumulative effect of all these measures is to prop up and perpetuate the artificial and decaying policy of the supremacy of the White man. The attitude of the Government to us is this:

'Let's beat them down with guns and batons and trample them under our feet. We must be ready to drown the whole country in blood if only there is the slightest chance of preserving White supremacy.' But there is nothing inherently superior about the *herrenvolk* idea of the supremacy of the Whites.

In China, India, Indonesia, and Korea, American, British, Dutch, and French imperialism, based on the concept of the supremacy of Europeans over Asians, has been completely and perfectly exploded. In Malaya and Indo-China, British and French imperialisms are being shaken to the foundations by powerful and revolutionary national liberation movements. In Africa there are approximately 190,000,000 Africans as against 4,000,000 Europeans.

The entire continent is seething with discontent, and already there are powerful revolutionary eruptions in the Gold Coast, Nigeria, Tunisia, Kenya, the Rhodesias, and South Africa. The oppressed people and the oppressors are at loggerheads. The day of reckoning between the forces of freedom and those of reaction is not far off. I have not the slightest doubt that when that day comes truth and justice will prevail. The intensification of repression and the extensive use of its bans is designed to immobilize every active worker and to check the national liberation movement. But gone are the days when harsh and wicked laws provided the oppressors with years of peace and quiet. The racial policies of the Government have pricked the conscience of all men of goodwill and has aroused their deepest indignation. The feelings of the oppressed people have never been more bitter. If the ruling circles seek to maintain their position by such inhuman methods then a clash between the forces of freedom and those of reaction is certain. The grave plight of the people compels them to resist to the death the stinking policies of the gangsters that rule our country. But in spite of all the difficulties outlined above, we have won important victories.

The general political level of the people has been considerably raised and they are now more conscious of their strength. Action has become the language of the day. The ties between the working people and the Congress have been greatly strengthened. This is a development of the highest importance because in a country such as ours a political organization that does not receive the support of the workers is in fact paralysed on the very ground on which it has chosen to wage battle.

Leaders of trade union organizations are at the same time important officials of the provincial and local branches of the African National Congress. In the past we talked of the African, Indian, and Coloured struggles. Though certain individuals raised the question of a united front of all the oppressed groups, the various non-European organizations stood miles apart from one another and the efforts of those for coordination and unity were like a voice crying in the wilderness; it seemed that the day would never dawn when the oppressed people would stand and fight together shoulder to shoulder against the common enemy.

Today we talk of the struggle of the oppressed people which, though it is waged through their respective autonomous organizations, is gravitating towards one central command. Our immediate task is to consolidate these victories to preserve our organizations, and to muster our forces for the resumption of the offensive. To achieve this important task the national executive of the African National Congress in consultation with the National Action Committee of the ANC and the South African Indian Congress formulated a plan of action popularly known as the 'M' Plan. The highest importance is attached to it by the national executive. Instructions were given to all provinces to implement the 'M' Plan without delay. The underlying principle of this plan is the understanding that it is no longer possible to wage our struggle mainly by the old methods of public meetings and printed circulars. The aim is:

To consolidate the Congress machinery.
To enable the transmission of the important decisions taken on a national level to every member of the organization without calling public meetings, issuing Press statements and printing circulars.
To build up in the local branches themselves local congresses which will effectively represent the strength and will of the people.
To extend and strengthen the ties between the Congress and the people and consolidate Congress leadership.

I appeal to all members of the Congress to redouble their

NO EASY WALK TO FREEDOM   29

efforts and play their part truly and well in its implementation. The hard and strenuous task of recruiting members and strengthening our organization through a house-to-house campaign in every locality must be done by you all.

From now on the activity of the Congressites must not be confined to speeches and resolutions. Their activities must find expression in wide-scale work among the masses, work which will enable them to make the greatest possible contact with the working people. You must protect and defend your trade unions. If you are not allowed to have your meetings publicly, then you must hold them over your machines in the factories, on the trains and buses as you travel home. You must have them in your villages and shanty-towns. You must make every home and every shack and every mud structure where our people live a branch of the trade union movement, and you must never surrender.

You must defend the right of the African parents to decide the kind of education that shall be given to their children. Teach the children that the Africans are not one iota inferior to Europeans. Establish your own community schools where the right kind of education will be given to our children. If it becomes dangerous or impossible to have these alternative schools, then again you must make every home, every shack or rickety structure a centre of learning for our children.

Never surrender to the inhuman and barbaric theories of Verwoerd. The decision to defy the unjust laws enabled Congress to develop considerably wider contacts between itself and the masses and the urge to join Congress grew day by day. But due to the fact that the local branches did not exercise proper control and supervision, the admission of new members was not carried out satisfactorily. No careful examinations were made of their past history and political characteristics. As a result of this there were many shady characters ranging from political clowns, place-seekers, splitters, saboteurs, *agents-provocateurs* to informers and even policemen who infiltrated into the ranks of Congress. One need only refer to the Johannesburg trial of Dr Moroka and nineteen others, where a member of Congress who actually worked at the national headquarters turned out to be a detective-sergeant on special duty. Remember the case of Leballo of Brakpan who wormed himself into that branch by producing faked letters . . . who had instructions to spy on us. There are many other similar instances that emerged during the Johannesburg, Port Elizabeth, and Kimberley trials. Whilst some of these men were discovered there are many who have not been found out. Outside appearances are highly deceptive, and we cannot classify these men by looking at their faces or listening to their sweet tongues, or by their vehement speeches demanding immediate action.

The friends of the people are distinguishable by the ready and disciplined manner in which they rally behind their organizations, and their readiness to sacrifice when the preservation of the organization has become a matter of life and death. Similarly, enemies and shady characters are detected by the extent to which they consistently attempt to wreck the organization by creating fratricidal strife, disseminating confusion, and undermining and even opposing important plans of action to vitalize the organization.

The presence of such elements in Congress constitutes a serious threat to the struggle, for the capacity for political action of an organization which is ravaged by such disruptive and splitting elements is considerably undermined. Here in South Africa, as in many parts of the world, a revolution is maturing: it is the profound desire, the determination and the urge of the overwhelming majority of the country to destroy forever the shackles of oppression that condemn them to servitude and slavery.

To overthrow oppression has been sanctioned by humanity and is the highest aspiration of every free man. If elements in our organization seek to impede the realization of this lofty purpose then these people have placed themselves outside the organization and must be put out of action before they do more harm. To do otherwise would be a crime and serious neglect of duty. We must rid ourselves of such elements and give our organization the striking power of a real militant mass organization. Kotane, Marks, Bopape, Tloome, and I have been banned from attending gatherings and we cannot join and counsel with you on the serious problems that are facing our country. We have been banned because we champion the freedom of the oppressed people of our country and because we consistently fought against the policy of racial discrimination in favour of a policy which accords fundamental human rights to all irrespective of race, colour, sex, or language. We are exiled from our own people for we uncompromisingly resisted the efforts of imperialist America and her satellites to drag the world into the rule of violence and brutal force, into the rule of the napalm, hydrogen, and cobalt bombs where millions of people will be wiped out to satisfy the criminal and greedy appetites of the imperialist powers. We have been gagged because we emphatically and openly condemned the criminal attacks by the imperialists against the people of Malaya, Vietnam, Indonesia, Tunisia, and Tanganyika and called upon our people to identify themselves unreservedly with the cause of world peace, and to fight against the war policies of America and her satellites.

We are being shadowed, hounded, and trailed because we fearlessly voiced our horror and indignation at the slaughter of the people of Korea and Kenya, because we expressed our solidarity with the cause of the Kenya people.

You can see that 'there is no easy walk to freedom anywhere and many of us will have to pass through the valley of the shadow of death again and again before we reach the mountain tops of our desires'.* Dangers and difficulties have not deterred us in the past; they will not frighten us now. But we must be prepared for them like men who mean business and who do not waste energy in vain talk and idle action. The way of preparation for action lies in our rooting out all impurity and indiscipline from our organization and making it the bright and shining instrument that will cleave its way to Africa's freedom.

1953

---

* Mandela quotes here from an article by Nehru 'From Lucknow to Tripoli' reprinted in *The Unity of India*.

2

FOLLOWING the Defiance Campaign the Government arraigned numbers of Congress leaders on charges under the Suppression of Communism Act. Presiding over the court in which Mandela and others were tried was Mr Justice Rumpff who eight years later was to be the senior judge in the Treason Trial when Mandela again stood in the dock. The sentence in the Defiance Campaign case was a suspended one of nine months, the judge commenting that the charge had 'nothing to do with communism as it is commonly known'.

In the years that followed Government bans on Mandela were renewed and extended. The Government could not take the risk of letting the people experience his qualities of leadership and so he was prohibited from making any public appearance or declaration. He began to write, and the result was the series of articles published in the journal *Liberation*, a Congress-supporting monthly run by former trade unionist and Congress executive member Dan Tloome. The articles appeared from June 1953 to May 1959.

The Defiance Campaign had made a tremendous impact on the African people. It had its effects, too, among sections of the Whites. In response to African demands asserted by defiance acts, two White bodies had been formed, the Congress of Democrats, which supported the aims of the African National Congress, and the Liberal Party.

The old debate broke out again. Votes for all, or the franchise for educated, 'civilized' men? Was half a loaf better than none? Would Africans win sympathy by showing moderation? Could change come through the all-White Parliament?

Many liberals and progressives among the Whites stirred to the African challenge but could not bring themselves to advocate one man one vote. Mandela regarded the stress on constitutionalism and the advocacy of the qualified franchise as an attack on the ANC's 1949 Programme of Action. He wrote an article attacking these policies, directing his fire at the first constitution of the Liberal Party, which that party was soon to change and then itself take part in extra-parliamentary action.

THE SHIFTING SANDS OF ILLUSION

THE Liberal Party constitution purports to uphold the 'essential dignity of every human being irrespective of race, colour, or creed, and the maintenance of his fundamental rights'. It expresses itself in favour of the 'right of every human being to develop to the fullest extent of which he is capable consistent with the rights of others'.

The new party's statement of principles thus far contents itself with the broad generalizations without any attempt to interpret them or define their practical application in the South African context. It then proceeds to announce 'that no person (should) be debarred from participation in the government or other democratic processes of the country by reason only of race, colour, or creed'. But here the neo-Liberals abandon the safe ground of generalization and stipulate explicitly 'that political rights based on a common franchise roll be extended to all SUITABLY QUALIFIED persons'. This question-begging formulation will not for long enable our Liberals to evade the fundamental issue: which persons are 'suitably qualified'?

The democratic principle is 'one adult, one vote'. The Liberals obviously differ from this well-known conception. They are, therefore, obliged to state an alternative theory of their own. This they have, so far, failed to do. The African National Congress, the South African Indian Congress, and the Congress of Democrats stand for votes for all: the demand, a century ago, of the British Chartists for universal equal franchise rights. Does the Liberal Party support this demand? Historical reality demands a plain and unequivocal answer . . .

In South Africa, where the entire population is almost split into two hostile camps in consequence of the policy of racial discrimination, and where recent political events have made the struggle between oppressor and oppressed even more acute, there can be no middle course. The fault of the Liberals—and this spells their doom—is to attempt to strike just such a course. They believe in criticizing and condemning the Government for its reactionary policies but they are afraid to identify themselves with the people and to assume the task of mobilizing that social force capable of lifting the struggle to higher levels.

The Liberal's credo states that to achieve their objects the party will employ 'only democratic and constitutional means and will oppose all forms of totalitarianism such as communism and fascism'. Talk of democratic and constitutional means can only have a basis in reality for those people who enjoy democratic and constitutional rights.

We must accept the fact that in our country we cannot win one single victory of political freedom without overcoming a desperate resistance on the part of the Government, and that victory will not come of itself but only as a result of a bitter struggle by the oppressed people for the overthrow of racial discrimination. This means that we are committed to struggle to mobilize from our ranks the forces capable of waging a determined and militant struggle against all forms of reaction. The theory that we can sit with folded arms and wait for a future parliament to legislate for the 'essential dignity of every human being irrespective of race, colour, or creed' is crass perversion of elementary principles of political struggle. No organization whose interests are identical with those of the toiling masses will advocate conciliation to win its demands.

To propose in the South African context that democrats limit themselves to constitutional means of struggle is to ask the people to submit to laws enacted by a minority parliament whose composition is essentially a denial of democracy to the over-whelming majority of the population. It means that we must obey a Constitution which debars the majority from participating in the government and other democratic processes of the country by reason only of race, colour, or creed. It implies in practice that we must carry passes and permit the violation of the essential dignity of a human being. It means that we must accept the Suppression of Communism Act which legalizes the gagging and persecution of leaders of the people because of their creed. It implies the acceptance of the Rehabilitation Scheme, the Bantu Authorities, the Group Areas, the Public Safety, the Criminal Law Amend-ments Act and all the wicked policies of the Government.

The real question is: in the general struggle for political rights can the oppressed people count on the Liberal Party as an ally?

The answer is that the new party merely gives organizational expression to a tendency which has for many years existed among a section of the White ruling class and in the United Party. This section hates and fears the idea of a revolutionary democracy in South Africa, just as much as the Malans* and the Oppenheimers† do. Rather than attempt the costly, dubious, and dangerous task of crushing the non-European mass movement by force, they would seek to divert it with fine words and promises and to divide it by giving concessions and bribes to a privileged minority (the 'suitably qualified' voters perhaps).

It becomes clear, therefore, that the high-sounding principles enunciated by the Liberal Party, though apparently democratic and progressive in form, are essentially reactionary in content. They stand not for the freedom of the people but for the adoption of more subtle systems of oppression and exploitation. Though they talk of liberty and human dignity they are subordinate henchmen of the ruling circles. They stand for the retention of the cheap labour system and of the subordinate colonial status of the non-European masses together with the Nationalist Government whose class interests are identical with theirs. In practice they acquiesce in the slavery of the people, low wages, mass unemployment, the squalid tenements in the locations and shanty-towns.

We of the non-European liberation movement are not racialists. We are convinced that there are thousands of honest democrats among the White population who are prepared to take up a firm and courageous stand for unconditional equality for the complete renunciation of 'White supremacy'. To them we extend the hand of sincere friendship and brotherly alliance. But no true alliance can be built on the shifting sands of evasions, illusions, and opportunism. We insist on presenting the conditions which make it reasonable to fight for freedom. The only sure road to this goal leads through the uncompromising and determined mass struggle for the overthrow of fascism and the establishment of democratic forms of government.

June 1953

* Dr Malan was South Africa's Prime Minister at this time—*Ed.*
† South Africa's leading mining magnate and financier who in 1953 was prominent in the United Party, the White parliamentary opposition —*Ed.*

LIVING UNDER APARTHEID

3

Editor's note

THE early 'fifties were a time of preparation for the first great coming together of all races of South Africans to work out their ideas for the future of their country.

The Congress of the People, held on 23 June 1955, was the culmination of a campaign to get the people—peasant and miner, housewife and domestic worker, trade unionist, taxi-driver and student, labourer and clerk—to speak out their demands for freedom. They wrote their conception of freedom in resolutions taken at unknown hundreds of meetings, then elected delegates to come in person to the mass conference that adopted the Freedom Charter.

The Freedom Charter said:

'South Africa belongs to all who live in it, black and white. No government can justly claim authority unless it is based on the will of all the people. . . .

'The people shall govern.

'All national groups shall have equal rights.

'The people shall share in the country's wealth.

'The land shall be shared among those who work it.

'All shall be equal before the law.

'All shall enjoy equal human rights.

'There shall be work and security.

'The doors of learning and culture shall be opened.

'There shall be houses, security, and comfort.

'There shall be peace and friendship.'

The simple popular demands were elaborated in full-length articles by Mandela and others.

PEOPLE ARE DESTROYED

RACHEL MUSI is fifty-three years of age. She and her husband had lived in Krugersdorp for thirty-two years. Throughout this period, he had worked for the Krugersdorp municipality for

£7 10s. a month. They had seven children ranging from nineteen to two years of age. One was doing the final year of the Junior Certificate at the Krugersdorp Bantu High School and three were in primary schools, also in Krugersdorp. She had several convictions for brewing kaffir beer. Because of these convictions she was arrested as an undesirable person in terms of the provisions of the Native Urban Areas Act and brought before the Additional Native Commissioner of Krugersdorp. After the arrest but before the trial her husband collapsed suddenly and died. Thereafter the Commissioner judged her an undesirable person and ordered her deportation to Lichtenburg. Bereaved and broken-hearted, and with the responsibility of maintaining seven children weighing heavily on her shoulders, an aged woman was exiled from her home and forcibly separated from her children to fend for herself among strangers in a strange environment . . .

In June 1952 I and about fifty other friends were arrested in Johannesburg while taking part in a defiance campaign and removed to Marshall Square. As we were being jostled into the drill yard one of our prisoners was pushed from behind by a young European constable so violently that he fell down some steps and broke his ankle. I protested, whereupon the young warrior kicked me on the leg in cowboy style. We were indignant and started a demonstration. Senior police officers entered the yard to investigate. We drew their attention to the injured man and demanded medical attention. We were curtly told that we could repeat our request the next day. And so it was that Samuel Makae spent a frightful night in the cells reeling and groaning with pain, maliciously denied medical assistance by those who had deliberately crippled him and whose duty it is to preserve and uphold the law.

In 1941 an African lad appeared before the Native Commissioner in Johannesburg charged with failing to give a good and satisfactory account of himself in terms of the above Act. The previous year he had passed the Junior Certificate with a few distinctions. He had planned to study Matric in the Cape but, because of illness, on the advice of the family doctor he decided to spend the year at home in Alexandra Township. Called upon by the police to produce proof that he had sufficient honest means of earning his livelihood, he explained that he was still a student and was maintained by his parents. He was then arrested and ordered to work at Leeuwkop Farm Colony for six months as an idle and disorderly person. This order was subsequently set aside on review by the Supreme Court but only after the young man had languished in jail for seven weeks, with serious repercussions to his poor health . . .

The breaking up of African homes and families and the forcible separation of children from mothers, the harsh treatment meted out to African prisoners, and the forcible detention of Africans in farm colonies for spurious statutory offences are a few examples of the actual workings of the hideous and pernicious doctrines of racial inequality. To these can be added scores of thousands of foul misdeeds committed against the people by the Government: the denial to the non-European people of the elementary rights of free citizenship; the expropriation of the people from their lands and homes to assuage the insatiable appetites of European land barons and industrialists; the flogging and calculated murder of African labourers by European farmers in the countryside for being 'cheeky to the baas'; the vicious manner in which African workers are beaten up by the police and flung into jails when they down tools to win their demands; the fostering of contempt and hatred for non-Europeans, the fanning of racial prejudice between whites and non-whites, between the various non-white groups; the splitting of Africans into small hostile tribal units; the instigation of one group or tribe against another; the banning of active workers from the people's organizations, and their confinement into certain areas.

All these misdemeanours are weapons resorted to by the mining and farming cliques of this country to protect their interests and to prevent the rise of an all-powerful organized mass struggle. To them, the end justifies the means, and that end is the creation of a vast market of cheap labour for mine magnates and farmers. That is why homes are broken up and people are removed from cities to the countryside to ensure enough labour for the farms. That is why non-European political opponents of the Government are treated with such brutality. In such a set-up, African youth with distinguished scholastic careers are not a credit to the country, but a serious threat to the governing circles, for they may not like to descend to the bowels of the earth and cough their lungs out to enrich the mining magnates, nor will they elect to dig potatoes on farms for wretched rations.

Nevertheless, these methods are failing to achieve their objective. True enough they have scared and deterred certain groups and individuals, and at times even upset and temporarily dislocated our plans and schemes. But they have not halted the growing struggle of the people for liberation. Capable fighters and organizers are arising from amongst the people. The people are increasingly becoming alive to the necessity of the solidarity of all democratic forces regardless of race, party affiliation, religious belief, and ideological conviction.

Taking advantage of this situation, the people's organizations have embarked on a broad programme of mutual co-operation and closer relations. The Freedom Charter recently adopted by people of all races and from all walks of life now forms the ground-plan for future action.

However, the fascist régime that governs this country is not meeting this situation with arms folded. Cabinet ministers are arming themselves with inquisitorial and arbitrary powers to destroy their opponents and hostile organizations. They are building a monoparty state, the essence of which is the identification of the Nationalist Party with State power. All opposition to the Nationalists has been deemed opposition to the State. Every facet of the national life is becoming subordinated to the overriding necessity of the party's retention of power. All constitutional safeguards are being thrown overboard and individual liberties are being ruthlessly suppressed. Lynchings and pogroms are the logical weapons to be resorted to, should the onward march of the liberation movement continue to manifest itself.

The spectre of Belsen and Buchenwald is haunting South Africa. It can only be repelled by the united strength of the people of South Africa. Every situation must be used to raise the people's level of understanding. If attacks on the people's organizations, if all discriminatory measures, be they the Industrial Conciliation Amendment Act, Bantu Education, or the classification of the Coloured people, are used as a rallying point around which a united front will be built, the spectre of Belsen and Buchenwald will never descend upon us.

October 1955

4

Editor's note

THE Transkei, Mandela's home, is South Africa's largest peasant Reserve but a centre of acute land hunger and peasant dissatisfaction. This article discusses the problem of organizing the peasants in the countryside.

LAND HUNGER

THE Transkeian Territories cover an area of more than 4,000,000 morgen of land, exclusive of trading sites and towns, with an African population of over 3,000,000. In comparison with the other so-called Native Reserves, this area is by far the largest single Reserve in the Union and also the greatest single reservoir of cheap labour in the country. According to official estimates, more than one-third of the total number of Africans employed on the Witwatersrand gold mines come from the Transkei.

It is thus clear that this area is the greatest single support of the most vicious system of exploitation—the gold mines. The continued growth and development of gold-mining in South Africa brought about by the discovery of gold in the Orange Free State calls for more and more of this labour at a time when the Union loses about 10,000 workers a year to the Central African Federation.

This labour problem compels South African mining circles to focus their attention more and more on the Reserves in a desperate effort to coerce every adult male African to seek employment on the mines. Recruiting agents are no longer content with discussing matters with chiefs and headmen only, as they have done in days gone by. Kraals, drinking parties, and initiation ceremonies are given particular attention and kraal-heads and tribesmen told that fame and fortune await them if they sign up their mine contracts. Films portraying a rosy picture of conditions on the mines are shown free of charge in the villages and rural locations.

But just in case these somewhat peaceful methods of persuasion fail to induce enough recruits, the authorities have in reserve more draconian forms of coercion. The implementation of the so-called rehabilitation scheme, the enforcement of taxes, and the foisting of tribal rule upon the people are resorted to in order to ensure a regular inflow of labour.

The rehabilitation scheme, which is the trump card of both the mining and the farming industries in this sordid game of coercion, was first outlined by Dr D. L. Smit, then Secretary for Native Affairs, at a special session of the General Council of the Ciskei held at Kingwilliamstown in January 1945. According to the Secretary's statement the scheme had two important features, namely, the limitation of stock to the carrying capacity of the land and the replanning of the Reserves to enable the inhabitants to make the best possible use of the land.

The main object of replanning, the statement continued, would be to demarcate residential, arable, and grazing areas in order that each portion of land should be used for the purpose to which it is best suited. Rural villages would be established to provide suitable homes for the families of Africans regularly employed in industrial and other services and, therefore, unable to make efficient use of a normal allotment of land.

In point of fact, the real purpose of the scheme is to increase land hunger for the masses of the peasants in the reserves and to impoverish them. The main object is to create a huge army of migrant labourers, domiciled in rural locations in the reserves far away from the cities. Through the implementation of the scheme it is hoped that in course of time the inhabitants of the reserves will be uprooted and completely severed from their land, cattle, and sheep, to depend for their livelihood entirely on wage earnings.

By enclosing them in compounds at the centres of work and housing them in rural locations when they return home, it is hoped to prevent the emergence of a closely knit, powerful, militant, and articulate African industrial proletariat who might acquire the rudiments of political agitation and struggle. What is wanted by the ruling circles is a docile, spineless, unorganized, and inarticulate army of workers.

Another method used to coerce African labour is the poll tax, also known as the general tax. When Cecil Rhodes introduced it in the old Cape Colony he openly and expressly declared that its main object would be to ensure cheap labour for industry, an object which has not changed since. In 1939, Parliament decided to make all African tax defaulters work for it, and the then Minister of Finance expressed the view that farmers would benefit through this arrangement. The extent of this benefit is clearly revealed by reference to statistics. According to the 1949 official Year Book for the Union, 21,381 Africans were arrested that year for general tax. Earlier, John Burger had stated in *The Black Man's Burden* that something like 60,000 arrests were made each year for non-payment of this tax. Since the Nationalist Party came to power these arrests have been intensified. In the Reserves, chiefs, headmen, mounted police, and court messengers comb the countryside daily for tax defaulters and, fearing arrest, thousands of Africans are forced to trek to the mines and surrounding farms in search of work. Around the jails in several parts of the country, queues of farmers are to be observed waiting for convicts.

Much has been written already on the aims and objects of the Bantu Authorities Act and on the implications of its acceptance by the Transkeian Bunga. Here we need only reiterate that reversion to tribal rule might isolate the democratic leadership from the masses and bring about the destruction of that leadership as well as of the liberation organizations. It will also act as a delaying tactic. In course of time the wrath of the people will be directed, it is hoped, not at the oppressor but at the Bantu Authorities who will be burdened with the dirty work of manipulating the detestable rehabilitation scheme, the collection of taxes, and the other measures which are designed to keep down the people.

It is clear, therefore, that the ruling circles attach the greatest importance to the Transkeian Territories. It is equally clear that the acceptance of tribal rule by the Bunga will henceforth be used by the Government to entice other tribal groups to accept the Act. As a matter of fact, this is precisely what the chiefs were told by

Government spokesmen at the Zululand and Rustenburg Indabas.*
Yet by a strange paradox the Transkei is the least politically
organized area in the Union. The Transkeian Organized Bodies
Association, once a powerful organization, is for all practical
purposes virtually defunct. The Cape African Teachers' Associa-.
tion is dominated by a group of intellectual snobs who derive
their inspiration from the All-African Convention. They are
completely isolated and have no influence whatsoever with the
masses of the people.

Recently when the African National Congress declared for a
boycott of Bantu Education and advocated the withdrawal of
children from such schools, the AAC fought against the withdrawal
and placed itself in the ridiculous position of opposing a boycott it
had pretended to preach all along. This somersault completely
exposed their opportunism and bankruptcy and the volume of
criticism now being directed against them has temporarily
silenced even the verbal theatricals for which they are famous.

Nevertheless, it is perfectly clear that the people of the Transkei
are indignant. Isolated and sporadic insurrections have occurred
in certain areas directed mainly against the rehabilitation scheme.
Chiefs and headmen have been beaten up by their tribesmen and
court actions are being fought. But in the absence of an organized
peasant movement coordinating these isolated and sporadic
outbursts the impact of this opposition will not be sharply felt by
the authorities.

Once more the problem of organization in the countryside poses
itself as one of major importance for the liberatory movement.
Through the coordination of spontaneous and local demonstrations, and their raising to a political level, the beginnings will be
found of opposition to the policy of oppressing and keeping
backward the people of the Transkei. Then we can look forward
to the day when the Transkei will be not a Reserve of cheap labour,
but a source of strength to build a free South Africa.

February 1956

* Tribal consultations—*Ed*.

5

Editor's note

EDUCATION for ignorance is the description Africans have given the system of Bantu education. A Government commission laid down that Bantu education would 'equip the child for his future work and surroundings' and Dr Verwoerd amplified: 'There is no place for him (the African) in the European community above the level of certain forms of labour.' Apartheid hoped to entrench itself by dominating the minds of the children in the schools. The Bantu education scheme of the Government was no sooner laid down for primary and secondary schools than the open universities were ordered to close their doors to African students and indoctrination for inferiority was spread to this field of higher education.

THE DOORS ARE BARRED

THE Nationalist Government has frequently denied that it is a fascist Government inspired by the theories of the National-Socialist Party of Hitlerite Germany. Yet the declarations it makes, the laws it passes, and the entire policy it pursues clearly confirm this point. It is interesting to compare the colonial policy of the Hitlerite Government as outlined by the leading German theoreticians on the subject. Dr Gunther Hecht, who was regarded as an expert on colonial racial problems in the office of the German National-Socialist Party, published a pamphlet in 1938 entitled *The Colonial Question and Racial Thought* in which he outlined the racial principles which were to govern the future treatment of Africans in German colonies. He declared that the German Government would not preach equality between Africans and Europeans. Africans would under no circumstances be allowed to leave German colonies for Europe. No African would be allowed to become a German citizen. African schools would not be permitted to preach any 'European matter' as that would foster a belief among them that Europe was the peak of cultural development and they would thus lose faith in their own culture and background. Local culture would be fostered. Higher schools and universities would be closed to them. Special theatres, cinemas, and other places of amusement and recreation would be erected for them. Hecht concluded the pamphlet by pointing out that the programme of the German Government would stand in sharp contrast to the levelling and anti-racial teachings of equality of the western colonial powers.

In this country the Government preaches the policy of *baasskap* which is based on the supremacy in all matters of the Whites over the non-Whites. They are subjected to extremely stringent regulations both in regard to their movement within the country as well as in regard to overseas travel lest they should come into contact with ideas that are in conflict with the *herrenvolk* policies of the Government. Through the Bantu Authorities Act and similar measures the African people are being broken up into small tribal units, isolated one from the other, in order to prevent the rise and development of national consciousness amongst them and to foster a narrow and insulated tribal outlook.

During the parliamentary debate on the second reading of the Bantu Education Bill in September 1953, the Minister of Native Affairs, Dr H. F. Verwoerd, who studied in German universities, outlined the educational policy of his Government. He declared that racial relations could not improve if the wrong type of education was given to Africans. They could not improve if the result of African education was the creation of a frustrated people who, as a result of the education they received, had expectations in life which circumstances in South Africa did not allow to be fulfilled; when it created people who were trained for professions not open to them; when there were people amongst them who had received a form of cultural training which strengthened their desire for white-collar occupations. Above all, good racial relations could not exist when the education was given under the control of people who believed in racial equality. It was, therefore, necessary that African education should be controlled in such a way that it should be in accord with the policy of the State.

The Bantu Education Bill has now become law and it embodies all the obnoxious doctrines enunciated by the Minister in the parliamentary debate referred to above. An inferior type of education, known as Bantu education, and designed to relegate the Africans to a position of perpetual servitude in a baasskap society, is now in force in almost all African primary schools throughout the country and will be introduced in all secondary and high schools as from next year. The Separate Universities Education Bill, now before Parliament, is a step to extend Bantu education to the field of higher education.

In terms of this Bill the Minister is empowered to establish, maintain, and conduct university colleges for non-Whites. The students to be admitted to the university colleges must be approved by the Minister. As from January 1958, no non-White students who were not previously registered shall be admitted to a European university without the consent of the Minister. The Bill also provides for the transfer and the control and management of the University College of Fort Hare and of the medical school for Africans at Wentworth to the Government; all employees in these institutions will become Government employees.

The Minister can vest the control of Fort Hare in the Native Affairs Department. The Government is empowered to change the name of the college. For example, he can call it the HENDRIK FRENSCH VERWOERD University College for Bantu persons. The Minister is entitled to dismiss any member of the staff for misconduct, which includes public adverse comment upon the administration, and propagating ideas, or taking part in, or identifying himself with, any propaganda or activities calculated to impede, obstruct, or undermine the activities of any government department.

No mixed university in the country will be permitted to enrol new non-European students any more. The mixed English universities of Cape Town, Witwatersrand, and Rhodes will thus be compelled to fall in line with the Afrikaans universities of Pretoria, Potchefstroom, Stellenbosch, and the Orange Free State whose doors are closed to non-Europeans.

The main purpose of the Bill is to extend the principle of Bantu education to the field of higher education. Non-Europeans who are trained at mixed universities are considered a menace to the racial policies of the Government. The friendship and inter-racial harmony that is forged through the admixture and associa-tion of various racial groups at the mixed universities constitute a direct threat to the policy of apartheid and baasskap and the Bill has been enacted to remove this threat. The type of universities the Bill envisages will be nothing more than tribal colleges, controlled by party politicians and based upon the doctrine of the perpetual supremacy of the Whites over the Blacks. Such colleges would be used by the Government to enforce its political ideology at a university level.

They will bear no resemblance whatsoever to modern uni-versities. Not free inquiry but indoctrination is their purpose, and the education they will give will not be directed towards the unleashing of the creative potentialities of the people but towards preparing them for perpetual mental and spiritual servitude to the Whites. They will be permitted to teach only that which strictly conforms to the racial policies of the Nationalist Govern-ment. Degrees and diplomas obtained at these colleges will be held in contempt and ridicule throughout the country and abroad and will probably not be recognized outside South Africa. The decision of the Government to introduce university segregation is prompted not merely by the desire to separate non-European from European students. Its implications go much further than this, for the Bill is a move to destroy the 'open' university tradition which is universally recognized throughout the civilized world and which has up to now been consistently practised by leading universities in the country for years. For centuries universities have served as centres for the dissemination of learning and knowledge to all students irrespective of their colour or creed. In multi-racial societies they serve as centres for the development of the cultural and spiritual aspects of the life of the people. Once the Bill is passed our universities can no longer serve as centres for the development of the cultural and spiritual aspects of the entire nation.

The Bill has aroused extensive and popular indignation, and opposition throughout the country as well as abroad. Students and lecturers, liberals and conservatives, progressives, democrats, public men and women of all races and with varying political affiliations, have been stirred into action. A former Chief Justice

of the Union, Mr Van der Sandt Centlivres, in a speech delivered
at a lunch meeting of the University Club in Cape Town on
11 February this year and reported in the *Rand Daily Mail* of
the 12th of the same month, said:

'I am not aware of any university of real standing in the outside world
which closes its doors to students on the ground of the colour of their
skins. The great universities of the world welcome students from other
countries whatever the colour of their skins. They realize that the
different outlook which these students bring with them advances the
field of knowledge in human relations in the international sphere and
contributes to their own culture.'

The attack on university freedom is a matter of vital importance
and constitutes a grave challenge to all South Africans. It is
perhaps because they fully appreciate this essential fact that more
people are participating in the campaign against the introduction
of academic segregation in the universities. Students in different
parts of the country are staging mammoth demonstrations and
protest meetings. Heads of universities, lecturers, men and women
of all shades of opinion, have in speeches and articles violently
denounced the action of the Government. All this reveals that
there are many men and women in this country who are prepared
to rally to the defence of traditional rights whenever they are
threatened.

But we cannot for one moment forget that we are up against a
fascist Government which has built up a massive coercive State
apparatus to crush democracy in this country and to silence the voice
of all those who cry out against the policy of apartheid and baasskap.
All opposition to the Nationalist Government is being ruthlessly
suppressed through the Suppression of Communism Act and
similar measures. The Government, in defiance of the people's
wishes, is deporting people's leaders from town and country in the
most merciless and shameful manner. All rights are being system-
atically attacked. The right to organize, to assemble, and to agitate
has been severely fettered. Trade unions and other organizations
are being smashed up. Even the sacred right of freedom of
religious worship, which has been observed and respected by
governments down the centuries, is now being tampered with.
And now the freedom of our universities is being seriously

threatened. Racial persecution of the non-Whites is being intensified every day. The rule of force and violence, of terror and
coercion, has become the order of the day.

Fascism has become a living reality in our country and its
defeat has become the principal task of the entire people of South
Africa. But the fight against the fascist policies of the Government
cannot be conducted on the basis of isolated struggles. It can only
be conducted on the basis of the united fight of the entire people
of South Africa against all attacks of the Nationalists on traditional
rights whether these attacks are launched through Parliament
and other State organs or whether through extra-parliamentary
forms. The more powerful the resistance of the people the less
becomes the advance of the Nationalists. Hence the importance
of a united front. The people must fight stubbornly and tenaciously
and defend every democratic right that is being attacked or
tampered with by the Nationalists.

A broad united front of all the genuine opponents of the racial
policies of the Government must be developed. This is the path
the people should follow to check and repel the advance of
fascism in this country and to pave the way for a peaceful and
democratic South Africa.

June 1957

THE FIGHT AGAINST
APARTHEID: OUR TACTICS
AND THEIRS

6

Editor's note

THE Freedom Charter was the first policy document to set out objectives for a non-racial democratic South Africa. It was more, wrote
Mandela, than a mere list of democratic reforms; it was a revolutionary
programme. It was not a socialist programme for it did not envisage the
transfer of power to any one social class, but it recognized that without
basic changes, like the nationalization of the mines, there could be no
over-all improvement in the conditions of the people and no democratic
system of government.

FREEDOM IN OUR LIFETIME

THE adoption of the Freedom Charter by the Congress of the
People was widely recognized both at home and abroad as an
event of major political significance in the life of this country. In
his message to the COP, Chief A. J. Lutuli, the banned National
President of the African National Congress, declared:

'Why will this assembly be significant and unique? Its size, I hope,
will make it unique. But above all its multi-racial nature and its noble
objectives will make it unique, because it will be the first time in the
history of our multi-racial nation that its people from all walks of life
will meet as equals, irrespective of race, colour, and creed, to formulate
a freedom charter for all people in the country.'

The COP was the most spectacular and moving demonstration
this country has ever seen; through it the people have given proof
that they have the ability and the power to triumph over every
obstacle and win the future of their dreams. Alfred Hutchinson,
reporting on the COP, coined the magnificent title 'A NEW WORLD

UNFOLDS . . .' which accurately summarized the political significance of that historic gathering.

The same theme was taken up by *Liberation* of September
last year when, in its editorial comment, it predicted that the
textbooks of the future would treat the Kliptown meeting as one
of the most important landmarks in our history. John Hatch, the
Public Relations Officer of the British Labour Party, in an article
published in the *New Statesman and Nation* of 28 January 1956,
under the title 'The Real South African Opposition', conceded
that some degree of success was achieved by the Congress movement when it approved the Charter. Finally, in his May Day
message published in *New Age*, Moses Kotane reviewed the
political achievements of 1955 and came to the conclusion that
the most outstanding one was the COP which produced the
world-renowned document—the Freedom Charter—which serves
as a beacon to the Congress Movement and an inspiration to the
people of South Africa.

Few people will deny, therefore, that the adoption of the
Charter is an event of major political significance in the life of
this country. The intensive and nation-wide political campaigning
that preceded it, the 2,844 elected delegates of the people that
attended, the attention it attracted far and wide and the favourable
comment it continues to receive at home and abroad from people
of divers political opinions and beliefs long after its adoption, are
evidence of this fact.

Never before has any document or conference been so widely
acclaimed and discussed by the democratic movement in South
Africa. Never before has any document or conference constituted
such a serious and formidable challenge to the racial and anti-
popular policies of the country. FOR THE FIRST TIME IN THE
HISTORY OF OUR COUNTRY THE DEMOCRATIC FORCES IRRE-
SPECTIVE OF RACE, IDEOLOGICAL CONVICTION, PARTY
AFFILIATION OR RELIGIOUS BELIEF HAVE RENOUNCED AND
DISCARDED RACIALISM IN ALL ITS RAMIFICATIONS, CLEARLY
DEFINED THEIR AIMS AND OBJECTS AND UNITED IN A
COMMON PROGRAMME OF ACTION.

The Charter is more than a mere list of demands for democratic
reforms. It is a revolutionary document precisely because the
changes it envisages cannot be won without breaking up the

economic and political set-up of present South Africa. To win
the demands calls for the organization, launching, and development of mass struggles on the widest scale. They will be won and
consolidated only as a result of a nation-wide campaign of agitation; through stubborn and determined mass struggles to defeat the
economic and political policies of the Nationalist Government; by re-
pulsing onslaughts on the living standards and liberties of the people.

The most vital task facing the democratic movement in this
country is to unleash such struggles and to develop them on the
basis of the concrete and immediate demands of the people from
area to area. Only in this way can we build a powerful mass
movement which is the only guarantee of ultimate victory in the
struggle for democratic reforms. Only in this way will the democratic movement become a vital instrument for the winning of
the democratic changes set out in the Charter.

Whilst the Charter proclaims democratic changes of a far-
reaching nature, it is by no means a blueprint for a socialist state
but a programme for the unification of various classes and groupings amongst the people on a democratic basis. Under socialism
the workers hold state power. They and the peasants own the
means of production, the land, the factories, and the mills. All
production is for use and not for profit. The Charter does not
contemplate such profound economic and political changes. Its
declaration 'The People Shall Govern!' visualizes the transfer of
power not to any single social class but to all the people of this
country, be they workers, peasants, professional men, or petty-
bourgeoisie.

It is true that in demanding the nationalization of the banks,
the gold mines, and the land, the Charter strikes a fatal blow at
the financial and gold-mining monopolies and farming interests
that have for centuries plundered the country and condemned its
people to servitude. But such a step is imperative because the
realization of the Charter is inconceivable, in fact impossible,
unless and until these monopolies are smashed and the national
wealth of the country turned over to the people. To destroy these
monopolies means the termination of the exploitation of vast
sections of the populace by mining kings and land barons and
there will be a general rise in the living standards of the people.
It is precisely because the Charter offers immense opportunities

for an overall improvement in the material conditions of all classes and groups that it attracts such wide support.

But a mere appraisal of a document, however dynamic its provisions or content might be, is academic and valueless unless we consciously and conscientiously create the conditions necessary for its realization. To be fruitful such appraisal must be closely linked up with the vital question of whether we have in South African society the requisite social forces that are capable of fighting for the realization of the Charter and whether in fact these forces are being mobilized and conditioned for this principal task.

The democratic struggle in South Africa is conducted by an alliance of various classes and political groupings amongst the non-European people supported by White democrats. African, Coloured, and Indian workers and peasants, traders and merchants, students and teachers, doctors and lawyers, and various other classes and groupings; all participate in the struggle against racial inequality and for full democratic rights. It was this alliance which launched the National Day of Protest on 26 June 1950. It was this alliance which unleashed the campaign for the defiance of unjust laws on 26 June 1952. It is this same alliance that produced the Freedom Charter. In this alliance the democratic movement has the rudiments of a dynamic and militant mass movement and, provided the movement exploits the initial advantages on its side at the present moment, immense opportunities exist for the winning of the demands in the Charter within our lifetime.

The striking feature about the population of our country and its occupational distribution is the numerical preponderance of the non-Europeans over Europeans and the economic importance of the former group in the key industries. According to the 1951 population census the population of the country consists of 2,643,000 Europeans as against 10,005,000 non-Europeans, a numerical disparity which is bound to have a decisive bearing on the final outcome of the present struggle to smash the colour-bar. According to the 1953 Official Year Book of the Union of South Africa there were 46,700 Europeans employed by the gold mines and collieries at the end of 1952. The number of Africans and Coloureds employed on the mines for the same period was 452,702, a proportion of 1 European employee to nearly 10 non-European employees. The racial composition of industrial employees in establishments with over ten employees during the period 1948–9 was as follows: Europeans 33 per cent; Africans 51·5 per cent; Asiatics 3 per cent; and Coloureds 12·5 per cent. According to the same Year Book, during 1952 there were 297,476 Europeans employed on farms occupied by Europeans and 2,188,712 Africans and 636,065 other non-Europeans.

The figures reveal the preponderant importance of the non-European people in the economic life of the country and the key task of the movement is to stimulate and draw these forces into the struggle for democratic reforms. A significant step was taken in Johannesburg on 3 March 1955, when a new trade union centre—the South African Congress of Trade Unions—was formed with delegates from thirty-four unions with a total membership of close on 42,000 and when for the first time in the history of trade unionism in South Africa, African, Coloured, European, and Indian workers united for a fighting policy on the basis of absolute equality. With 42,000 organized workers on our side and fighting under the flag of a trade union centre that has completely renounced racialism and committed itself to a militant and uncompromising policy, it remains for us to redouble our efforts and carry our message to every factory and mill throughout the country. The message of the new centre is bound to attract the support of the majority of the workers for they have no interest whatsoever in the country's policy of racial discrimination.

The workers are the principal force upon which the democratic movement should rely, but to repel the savage onslaughts of the Nationalist Government and to develop the fight for democratic rights it is necessary that the other classes and groupings be joined. Support and assistance must be sought and secured from the 452,702 African and Coloured mine-workers, from the 2,834,777 non-European labourers employed on European farms and from the millions of peasants that occupy the so-called Native Reserves of the Union. The cruel and inhuman manner with which they are treated, their dreadful poverty and economic misery, make them potential allies of the democratic movement.

The non-European traders and businessmen are also potential allies, for in hardly any other country in the world has the ruling class made conditions so extremely difficult for the rise of a non-European middle class as in South Africa. The law of the country prohibits non-Europeans from owning or possessing minerals. Their right to own and occupy land is very much restricted and circumscribed and it is virtually impossible for them to own factories and mills. Therefore they are vitally interested in the liberation of the non-European people, for it is only by destroying White supremacy and through the emancipation of the non-Europeans that they can prosper and develop as a class. To each of these classes and groups the struggle for democratic rights offers definite advantages. To every one of them the realization of the demands embodied in the Charter would open a new career and vast opportunities for development and prosperity. These are the social forces whose alliance and unity will enable the democratic movement to vanquish the forces of reaction and win the democratic changes envisaged in the Charter.

In the present political situation in South Africa when the Nationalist Government has gone all out to smash the people's political organization and the trade union movement through the Suppression of Communism Act and its anti-trade union legislation, it becomes important to call upon and to stimulate every class to wage its own battles. It becomes even more important that all democratic forces be united and the opportunities for such a united front are growing every day. On 3 March 1955 a non-colour-bar trade union centre is formed. On 26 June the same year in the most spectacular and moving demonstration this country has ever seen, 2,844 delegates of the people adopt the Charter, and four months thereafter more than 1,000 women of all races stage a protest march to Pretoria to put their demands to the Government—all this in the course of one year.

The rise of the Congress movement and the powerful impact it exerts on the political scene in the country is due precisely to the fact that it has consistently followed and acted on the vital policy of democratic unity. It is precisely because of the same reason that the Congress movement is rapidly becoming the real voice of South Africa. If this united front is strengthened and developed the Freedom Charter will be transformed into a dynamic and living instrument and we shall vanquish all opposition and win the South Africa of our dreams during our lifetime.

June 1956

7

ALL these years Mandela was banned from gatherings and under constant police surveillance, but he continued to lead in the shadows of small and select Congress meetings. By now there was a strong working alliance of the Congress movement, headed by the ANC and consisting of the Congresses of the Indian people and the Coloured people, the S.A. Congress of Trade Unions, and the Congress of Democrats. The tactic of boycott came under scrutiny and Mandela wrote on it.

OUR STRUGGLE NEEDS MANY TACTICS

POLITICAL organizations in this country have frequently employed the boycott weapon in their struggle against racial discrimination and oppression. In 1947 the African National Congress decided to boycott all elections under the Native Representatives Act of 1936, as well as all elections to the United Transkeian Territories General Council, generally referred to as the Bunga; to the Advisory Boards and all other discriminatory statutory institutions specially set up for Africans. A year earlier the South African Indian Congress had decided to boycott and had launched a resistance campaign against the Asiatic Land Tenure and Indian Representation Act which, *inter alia*, made special provision for the representation in Parliament of Indians in the Provinces of Natal and the Transvaal and for the representation in the Provincial Council of Natal of Indians in that Province. In 1957 the South African Coloured People's Organization (SACPO) considered its attitude on the question of the election of four Europeans to represent the Coloured people in Parliament and decided to boycott these elections as well as the election of twenty-seven

Coloured persons to the Union Council of Coloured Affairs. The same year SACPO reversed this decision and decided to participate in the parliamentary elections.

Apart from such boycotts of unrepresentative institutions, boycotts of a different kind have often been called by various organizations on matters directly affecting the people. For example in 1949 the Western Areas Tram Fares Committee successfully boycotted the increased fares on the Johannesburg–Western Areas tram route. Similarly last year, and by means of the boycott weapon, the Alexandra People's Transport Committee achieved a brilliant victory when it rebuffed and defeated the decision of the Public Utility Transport Corporation, backed by the Government, to increase fares along the Johannesburg–Alexandra bus route. The Federation of South African Nurses and Midwives is presently campaigning for the boycott of all discriminatory provisions of the Nursing Amendment Act passed last year. By and large, boycott is recognized and accepted by the people as an effective and powerful weapon of political struggle.

Perhaps it is precisely because of its effectiveness and the wide extent to which various organizations employ it in their struggles to win their demands that some people regard the boycott as a matter of principle which must be applied invariably at all times and in all circumstances irrespective of the prevailing conditions. This is a serious mistake, for the boycott is in no way a matter of principle but a tactic weapon whose application should, like all other political weapons of the struggle, be related to the concrete conditions prevailing at the given time.

For example, the boycott by the Indian community of the representation machinery contained in the Asiatic Land Tenure and Indian Representation Act of 1946 was correct at the time not because the boycott is a correct principle but because the Indian people correctly gauged the objective situation. Firstly, the political concessions made in the Act were intended to bribe the Indian people to accept the land provisions of this Act which deprived the Indians of their land rights—a bribe which even the Indian reactionaries were not prepared to accept. Secondly, a remarkable degree of unity and solidarity had been achieved by the Indian people in their struggle against the Act. The conservative Kajee-Pather *bloc* worked in collaboration with the progressive and militant Dadoo-Naicker wing of the SAIC and no less than 35,000 members had been recruited into the SAIC before the commencement of the campaign. Under these conditions the boycott proved correct and not a single Indian person registered as a voter in terms of the Act.

Similarly, the 1947 boycott resolutions of the ANC was correct, in spite of the fact that no effective country-wide campaign was carried out to implement this resolution. It will be recalled that at the time, in an endeavour to destroy the people's political organizations and to divert them from these organizations, the United Party Government was fostering the illusion that the powers of the Natives Representation Council, the Bunga, the Advisory Boards, and similar institutions would be increased to such an extent that the African people would have an effective voice in the government of the country. The agitation that followed the adoption of the boycott resolution by the ANC, inadequate as it was, helped to damage the influence of these sham institutions and to discredit those who supported them. In certain areas these institutions were completely destroyed and they have now no impact whatsoever on the outlook of the people. To put the matter crisply, the 1947 resolution completely frustrated the scheme of the United Party Government to confuse the people and to destroy their political organization.

In some cases, therefore, it might be correct to boycott, and in others it might be unwise and dangerous. In still other cases another weapon of political struggle might be preferred. A demonstration, a protest march, a strike, or civil disobedience might be resorted to, all depending on the actual conditions at the given time.

In the opinion of some people, participation in the system of separate racial representation in any shape or form, and ir-respective of any reasons advanced for doing so, is impermissible on principle and harmful in practice. According to them such participation can only serve to confuse the people and to foster the illusion that they can win their demands through a parliamentary form of struggle. In their view the people have now become so politically conscious and developed that they cannot accept any form of representation which in any way fetters their progress. They maintain that people are demanding direct representation in

Parliament, in the provincial and city councils, and that nothing short of this will satisfy them. They say that leaders who talk of the practical advantages to be gained by participation in separate racial representation do not have the true interests of the people at heart. Finally, they argue that the so-called representatives have themselves expressed the view that they have achieved nothing in Parliament. Over and above this, the argument goes, the suggestion that anything could be achieved by electing such representatives to Parliament is made ridiculous by their paucity of numbers in Parliament. This view has been expressed more specifically in regard to the question of boycott of the forthcoming Coloured Parliamentary seats.

The basic error in this argument lies in the fact that it regards the boycott not as a tactical weapon to be employed if and when objective conditions permit but as an inflexible principle which must under no circumstances be varied. Having committed this initial mistake, people who advocate this point of view are invariably compelled to interpret every effort to relate the boycott to specific conditions as impermissible deviations on questions of principle. In point of fact, total and uncompromising opposition to racial discrimination in all its ramifications and refusal to cooperate with the Government in the implementation of its reactionary policies are matters of principle in regard to which there can be no compromise.

In its struggle for the attainment of its demands the liberation movement avails itself of various political weapons, one of which might (but not necessarily) be the boycott. It is, therefore, a serious error to regard the boycott as a weapon that must be employed at all times and in all conditions. In this stand there is also the failure to draw the vital distinction between participation in such elections by the people who accept racial discrimination and who wish to cooperate with the Government in the oppression and exploitation of their own people on the one hand, and participation in such elections, not because of any desire to cooperate with the Government but in order to exploit them in the interest of the liberatory struggle on the other hand. The former is the course generally followed by collaborators and Government stooges and has for many years been consistently condemned and rejected by the liberal movement. The latter course, provided objective conditions permit, serves to strengthen the people's struggle against the reactionary policies of the Government.

The decision of SACPO in favour of participation in the forthcoming parliamentary elections is correct for various reasons. The principal and most urgent task facing the Congress movement today is the defeat of the Nationalist Government and its replacement by a less reactionary one. Any step or decision which helps the movement to attain this task is politically correct. The election of four additional members to Parliament, provided they agree with the general aims of the movement and provided that they are anti-Nationalist, would contribute to the defeat of the present Government. In advocating this course it is not in any way being suggested that the salvation of the oppressed people of this country depends on the parliamentary struggle, nor is it being suggested that a United Party régime would bring about any radical changes in the political set-up in this country. It is accepted and recognized that the people of South Africa will win their freedom as a result of the pressure they put up against the reactionary policies of the Government. Under a United Party Government it will still be necessary to wage a full-scale war on racial discrimination. But the defeat of the Nationalists would at least lighten the heavy burden of harsh and restrictive legislation that is borne by the people at the present moment. There would be a breathing space during which the movement might recuperate and prepare for fresh assaults against the oppressive policies of the Government.

SACPO's struggle and influence amongst the Coloured people has grown tremendously, but it is not without opposition and there are still large numbers of Coloured people who are outside its fold. In order to succeed, a boycott would require a greater degree of unity and solidarity than has so far been achieved amongst the Coloured people. Prior to the December resolution certain Coloured organizations had indicated their willingness to participate in these elections. To boycott elections under such conditions might result in hostile and undesirable elements being returned to Parliament.

In several conferences of the ANC, both national and provincial, the view has been expressed that the 1947 boycott resolution requires to be reviewed in the light of the new conditions created as a result of the serious and dangerous attacks launched by the Nationalists on the liberation movement. The political situation has radically changed since. The political organizations of the people are functioning under the conditions of semi-illegality. Legal authorities are refusing to permit meetings within their areas and it is becoming increasingly difficult to hold conferences. Some of the most experienced and active members have been deported from their homes, others have been confined to certain areas, and many have been compelled to resign from their organizations.

The present Government regards institutions such as the Advisory Boards as too advanced and dangerous, and these are being replaced by tribal institutions under the Bantu Authorities Act. Platforms for the dissemination of propaganda are gradually disappearing. Having regard to the principal task of ousting the Nationalist Government, it becomes necessary for the Congress to review its attitude towards the special provision for the representation of Africans set out in the 1936 Act. The parliamentary forum must be exploited to put forth the case for a democratic and progressive South Africa. Let the democratic movement have a voice both outside and within Parliament. Through the Advisory Boards and, if the right type of candidates are found, through Parliament, we can reach the masses of the people and rally them behind us.

February 1958

8

Editor's note

REPRESSION was one arm of Nationalist Government policy. Raids, arrests, bannings, banishments, persecution of political leaders were to silence those who dared to speak for their people.

The other arm was a fake system of tribal self-government, the Bantustans. Africans were to be permitted certain limited rights, at the Government's pleasure, in their own areas. Bantustans were Dr Verwoerd's answer to world criticism of apartheid, part of a scheme aimed at disarming Western governments and investors. Above all, the creation of Bantustans was an attempt to blunt the sharp edge of African nationalism by fostering tribal divisions in the segregated backwater Reserves.

VERWOERD'S TRIBALISM

'South Africa belongs to all who live in it, black and white.'—Freedom Charter.

'All the Bantu have their permanent homes in the Reserves and their entry into other areas and into the urban areas is merely of a temporary nature and for economic reasons. In other words, they are admitted as work-seekers, not as settlers.'—Dr W. W. M. Eiselen, Secretary of the Department of Bantu Administration and Development. (Article in *Optima*, March 1959)

THE statements quoted above contain diametrically opposite conceptions of this country, its future, and its destiny. Obviously they cannot be reconciled. They have nothing in common, except that both of them look forward to a future of affairs rather than that which prevails at present. At present, South Africa does not 'belong'—except in a moral sense—to all.

Ninety-seven per cent of the country is legally owned by members (a handful of them at that) of the dominant White minority. And at present by no means 'all' Africans have their 'permanent homes' in the Reserves. Millions of Africans were born and have their permanent homes in the towns and cities and elsewhere outside the Reserves, have never seen the Reserves, and have no desire to go there.*

It is necessary for the people of this country to choose between these two alternative paths. It is assumed that readers of *Liberation* are familiar with the detailed proposals contained in the Charter.

Let us therefore study the policies submitted by the Nationalist Party.

The newspapers have christened the Nationalists' plan as one for 'Bantustans'. The hybrid word is, in many ways, extremely misleading. It derives from the partitioning of India after the reluctant departure of the British, and as a condition thereof, into two separate states, Hindustan and Pakistan. There is no real parallel with the Nationalists' proposals, for:

    (a) India and Pakistan constitute two completely separate and politically independent states.
    (b) Muslims enjoy equal rights in India; Hindus enjoy equal rights in Pakistan.
    (c) Partition was submitted to and approved by both parties, or at any rate fairly widespread and influential sections of each.

The Government's plans do not envisage the partitioning of this country into separate, self-governing states. They do not envisage equal rights, or any rights at all, for Africans outside the Reserves. Partition has never been approved of by Africans and never will be. For that matter it has never really been submitted to or approved of by the Whites. The term 'Bantustan' is therefore a complete misnomer, and merely tends to help the Nationalists perpetrate a fraud.

Let us examine each of these aspects in detail.

It is typical of the Nationalists' propaganda techniques that

---

* According to the 1951 census, trust land locations and Reserves accounted for only 2½ million out of a total African population of, at that time, 8½ million. A further 2½ million, nearly, were on European-owned farms. The rest were mainly in urban areas—*Ed*.

they describe their measures in misleading titles, which convey
the opposite of what the measures contain. Verwoerd called his
law greatly extending and intensifying the pass laws the 'Abolition
of Passes' Act. Similarly, he has introduced into the current
parliamentary session a measure called the 'Promotion of Bantu
Self-Government Bill'. It starts off by decreeing the abolition of
the tiny token representation of Africans (by Whites) in Parliament
and the Cape Provincial Council.

It goes on to provide for the division of the African population
into eight 'ethnic units' (the so-called Bantustans). They are:
North and South Sotho, Swazi, Tsonga, Tswana, Venda, Xhosa,
and Zulu. These units are to undergo a 'gradual development to
self-government'.

This measure was described by the Prime Minister, Dr
Verwoerd, as a 'supremely positive step' towards placing Africans
'on the road to self-government'. Mr De Wet Nel, Minister of
Bantu Affairs, said the people in the Reserves 'would gradually be
given more powers to rule themselves'.

The scheme is elaborated in a White Paper, tabled in the
House of Assembly, to 'explain' the Bill. According to this
document, the immediate objects of the Bill are:

(a) The recognition of the so-called Bantu National Units and
the appointment of Commissioners-General whose task will
be to give guidance and advice to the units in order to
promote their general development, with special reference
to the administrative field.

(b) The linking of Africans working in urban areas with
territorial authorities established under the Bantu Authorities Act, by conferring powers on the Bantu authorities
to nominate persons as their representatives in urban areas.

(c) The transfer to the Bantu territorial authorities, at the
appropriate time, of land in their areas at present held by
the Native Trust.

(d) The vesting in territorial Bantu authorities of legislative
authority and the right to impose taxes, and to undertake
works and give guidance to subordinate authorities.

(e) The establishments of territorial boards for the purpose of
temporary liaison through commissioners-general if during

the transition period the administrative structure in any area has not yet reached the stage where a territorial authority has been established.

(f) The abolition of representation in the highest European governing bodies.

According to the same White Paper, the Bill has the following further objects:

(a) The creation of homogeneous administrative areas for Africans by uniting the members of each so-called national group in the national unit, concentrated in one coherent homeland where possible.

(b) The education of Africans to a sound understanding of the problems of soil conversion and agriculture so that all rights over and responsibilities in respect of soil in African areas may be assigned to them.

   This includes the gradual replacement of European agricultural officers of all grades by qualified and competent Africans.

(c) The systematic promotion of a diverse economy in the African areas, acceptable to Africans and to be developed by them.

(d) The education of the African to a sound understanding of the problems and aims of Bantu education so that, by the decentralization of powers, responsibility for the different grades of education may be vested in them.

(e) The training of Africans with a view to effectively extending their own judicial system and their education to a sound understanding of the common law with a view to transferring to them responsibilities for the administration of justice in their areas.

(f) The gradual replacement of European administrative officers by qualified and competent Africans.

(g) The exercise of legislative powers by Africans in respect of their areas, at first at a limited scale, but with every intention of gradually extending this power.

It will be seen that the African people are asked to pay a very high price for this so-called 'self-government' in the Reserves. Urban Africans—the workers, businessmen, and professional men and women, who are the pride of our people in the stubborn and victorious march towards modernization and progress—are to be treated as outcasts, not even 'settlers' like Dr Verwoerd. Every vestige of rights and opportunities will be ruthlessly destroyed. Everywhere outside the Reserves an African will be tolerated only on condition that he is for the convenience of the Whites.

There will be forcible uprooting and mass removals of millions of people to 'homogeneous administrative areas'. The Reserves, already intolerably overcrowded, will be crammed with hundreds of thousands more people evicted by the Government.

In return for all these hardships, in return for Africans abandoning their birthright as citizens, pioneers, and inhabitants of South Africa, the Government promises them 'self-government' in the tiny 13 per cent that their greed and miserliness 'allocates' to us. But what sort of self-government is this that is promised?

There are two essential elements to self-government, as the term is used and understood all over the modern world. They are:

1 *Democracy*. The organs of government must be representative; that is to say, they must be freely chosen leaders and representatives of the people, whose mandate must be renewed at periodic democratic elections.
2 *Sovereignty*. The government thus chosen must be free to legislate and act as it deems fit on behalf of the people, not subject to any limitations upon its powers by any alien authority.

Neither of these two essentials is present in the Nationalist plan. The 'Bantu National Units' will be ruled in effect by the commissioners-general appointed by the Bantu Government, and administered by the Bantu Affairs Department officials under his control. When the Government says it plans gradually increasing self-government, it merely means that more powers in future will be exercised by appointed councils of chiefs and headmen. No provision is made for elections. The Nationalists say that chiefs, not elected legislatures, are 'the Bantu tradition'.

There was a time when, like all peoples on earth, Africans conducted their simple communities through chiefs, advised by tribal councils and mass meetings of the people. In those times the chiefs were indeed representative governors. Nowhere, however, have such institutions survived the complexities of modern industrial civilization. Moreover, in South Africa we all know full well that no chief can retain his post unless he submits to Verwoerd, and many chiefs who sought the interest of their people before position and self-advancement have, like President Lutuli, been deposed.

Thus, the proposed Bantu authorities will not be, in any sense of the term, representative or democratic.

The point is made with pride by the Bantu Affairs Department itself in an official publication:

'The councillors will perform their task without fear or prejudice, because they are not elected by the majority of votes, and they will be able to lead their people onwards . . . even though . . . it may demand hardships and sacrifices.'

A strange paean to autocracy, from a department of a Government which claims to be democratic!

In spite of all their precautions to see that their 'territorial authorities'—appointed themselves, subject to dismissal by themselves and under constant control by their commissioners-general and their Bantu Affairs Department—never become authentic voices of the people, the Nationalists are determined to see that even those puppet bodies never enjoy real power of sovereignty.

In his notorious (and thoroughly dishonest) article in *Optima*, Dr Eiselen draws a far-fetched comparison between the relations between the future 'Bantustans' and the Union Government, on the one hand, and those between Britain and the self-governing Dominions on the other. He foresees:

'A cooperative South African system based on the Commonwealth conception, with the Union Government gradually changing its position from guardian and trustee to become instead the senior member of a group of separate communities.'

To appreciate the full hypocrisy of this statement, it must be remembered that Dr Eiselen is an official of a Nationalist Party Government, a member of a party which has built its fortune for the past half century on its cry that it stands for full untrammelled sovereignty within the Commonwealth, that claims credit for Hertzog's achievements in winning the Statute of Westminster, which proclaims such sovereignty, and which even now wants

complete independence and a republic outside the Commonwealth.

It cannot be claimed, therefore, that Eiselen and Verwoerd do
not understand the nature of a commonwealth, or sovereignty, or
federation.

What are we to think, then, in the same article, when Dr
Eiselen comes into the open, and declares:

'The utmost degree of autonomy in administrative matters which the
Union Parliament is likely to be prepared to concede to these areas will
stop short of actual surrender of sovereignty by the European trustee,
and there is therefore no prospect of a federal system with eventual
equality among members taking the place of the South African Commonwealth . . .'

There is no sovereignty then. No autonomy. No democracy.
No self-government. Nothing but a crude, empty fraud, to bluff
the people at home and abroad, and to serve as a pretext for
heaping yet more hardships and injustices upon the African
people.

Politically, the talk about self-government for the Reserves is a
swindle. Economically, it is an absurdity.

The few scattered African Reserves in various parts of the
Union, comprising about 13 per cent of the least desirable land
area, represent the last shreds of land ownership left to the African
people of their original ancestral home. After the encroachments
and depredations of generations of European land-sharks,
achieved by force and by cunning, and culminating in the outrageous Land Act from 1913 onwards, had turned the once free
and independent Tswana, Sotho, Xhosa, Zulu, and other peasant
farmers of this country into a nation of landless outcasts and
roving beggars, humble 'work-seekers' on the mines and the
farms where yesterday they had been masters of the land, the new
White masters of the country 'generously presented' them the
few remaining miserable areas as reservoirs and breeding-grounds
for Black labour. These are the Reserves.

It was never claimed or remotely considered by the previous
governments of the Union that these Reserves could become
economically self-sufficient 'national homes' for 9,600,000 African
people of this country. The final lunacy was left to Dr Verwoerd,
Dr Eiselen, and the Nationalist Party.

The facts are—as every reader who remembers Govan Mbeki's brilliant series of articles on the Transkei in *Liberation* will be aware—that the Reserves are congested distressed areas, completely unable to sustain their present populations. The majority of the adult males are always away from home working in the towns, mines, or European-owned farms. The people are on the verge of starvation.

The White Paper speaks of teaching Africans soil conservation and agriculture and replacing European agricultural officers by Africans. This is merely trifling with the problem. The root problem of the Reserves is the intolerable congestion which already exists. No amount of agricultural instruction will ever enable 13 per cent of the land to sustain 66 per cent of the population.

The Government is, of course, fully aware of the fact. They have no intention of creating African areas which are genuinely self-supporting (and which could therefore create a genuine possibility for self-government). If such areas were indeed self-supporting, where would the Chamber of Mines and the Nationalist farmers get their supplies of cheap labour?

In the article to which I have already referred, Dr Eiselen bluntly admits:

'In fact not much more than a quarter of the community (on the Reserves) can be farmers, the others seeking their livelihood in industrial, commercial, professional, or administrative employment.'

Where are they to find such employment? In the Reserves? To anyone who knows these poverty-stricken areas, sadly lacking in modern communications, power-resources, and other needed facilities, the idea of industrial development seems far-fetched indeed. The beggarly £500,000 voted to the so-called 'Bantu Investment Corporation' by Parliament is mere eyewash: it would not suffice to build a single decent road, railway line, or power station.

The Government has already established a number of 'rural locations'—townships in the Reserves. The Eiselen article says a number more are planned: he mentions a total of no less than ninety-six. Since the residents will not farm, how will they manage to keep alive, still less pay rents and taxes and support the traders, professional classes, and civil servants whom the optimistic Eiselen envisages will make a living there?

Fifty-seven towns on the borders of the Reserves have been designated as centres where White capitalists can set up industries. Perhaps some will migrate, and thus 'export' their capital resources of cheap labour and land. Certainly, unlike the Reserves (which are a monument to the callous indifference of the Union Parliament to the needs of the non-voting African taxpayers), these towns have power, water, transport, railways, etc. The Nationalist Government, while it remains in office, will probably subsidize capitalists who migrate in this way. It is already doing so in various ways, thus creating unemployment in the cities. But it is unlikely that any large-scale voluntary movement will take place away from the big, established industrial centres, with their well-developed facilities, available materials, and markets.

Even if many industries were forced to move to the border areas around the Reserves it would not make one iota of difference to the economic viability of the Reserves themselves. The fundamental picture of the Union's economy could remain fundamentally the same as at present: a single integrated system based upon the exploitation of African labour by White capitalists.

Economically, the 'Bantustan' concept is just as big a swindle as it is politically.

Thus we find, if we really look into it, that this grandiose 'partition' scheme, this 'supremely positive step' of Dr Verwoerd, is like all apartheid schemes—high-sounding double-talk to conceal a policy of ruthless oppression of the non-Whites and of buttressing the unwarranted privileges of the White minority, especially the farming, mining, and financial circles.

Even if it were not so, however, even if the scheme envisaged a genuine sharing-out of the country on the basis of population figures, and a genuine transfer of power to elected representatives of the people, it would remain fundamentally unjust and dangerously unstable unless it were submitted to, accepted, and endorsed by all parties to the agreement. To think otherwise is to fly in the face of the principle of self-determination, which is upheld by all countries and confirmed in the United Nations Charter, to which this country is pledged.

Now even Dr Eiselen recognizes this difficulty to some extent.

He pays lip-service to the Atlantic Charter and appeals to 'Western democracy'. He mentions the argument that apartheid would only be acceptable 'provided that the parties concerned agreed to this of their own free will'. And then he most dishonestly evades the whole issue. 'There is no reason for ruling out apartheid on the grounds that the vast majority of the population oppose it,' he writes. 'The Bantu as a whole do not demand integration, in a single society. This is the idea . . . merely of a small minority.'

Even Dr Eiselen, however, has not the audacity to claim that the African people actually favour apartheid or partition.

Let us state clearly the facts of the matter, with the greatest possible clarity.

NO SERIOUS OR RESPONSIBLE LEADER, GATHERING, OR ORGANIZATION OF THE AFRICAN PEOPLE HAS EVER AC-CEPTED SEGREGATION, SEPARATION, OR THE PARTITION OF THIS COUNTRY IN ANY SHAPE OR FORM.

At Bloemfontein in 1956, under the auspices of the United African clergy, perhaps the most widely attended and representative gathering of African representatives, of every shade of political opinion ever held, unanimously and uncompromisingly rejected the Tomlinson Report, on which the Verwoerd plan is based, and voted in favour of a single society.

Even the rural areas, where dwell the 'good' (i.e. simple and ignorant) 'Bantu' of the imagination of Dr Verwoerd and Dr Eiselen, attempts to impose apartheid have met, time after time, with furious, often violent resistance. Chief after chief has been deposed or deported for resisting 'Bantu authorities' plans. Those who, out of short-sightedness, cowardice, or corruption, have accepted these plans have earned nothing but the contempt of their own people.

It is a pity that, on such a serious subject, and at such a crucial period, serious misstatements should have been made by some people who purport to speak on behalf of the Africans. For example, Mrs Margaret Ballinger, the Liberal Party M.P., is reported as saying in the Assembly 'no confidence' debate:

'The Africans have given their answer to this apartheid proposition but, of course, no one ever listens to them. They have said: "If you want separation then let us have it. Give us half of South Africa. Give us the eastern half of South Africa. Give us some of the developed resources because we have helped to develop them." ' (*S.A. Outlook*, March 1959)

It is most regrettable that Mrs Ballinger should have made such a silly and irresponsible statement towards, one fears, the end of a distinguished parliamentary career. For in this instance she has put herself in the company of those who do not listen to the Africans. No Africans of any standing have ever made the proposals put forward by her.

The leading organization of the African people is the African National Congress. Congress has repeatedly denounced apartheid. It has repeatedly endorsed the Freedom Charter, which claims South Africa 'for all its people'. It is true that occasionally individual Africans become so depressed and desperate at Nationalist misrule that they have tended to clutch at any straw to say: give us any little corner where we may be free to run our own affairs. But Congress has always firmly rejected such momentary tendencies and refused to barter our birthright, which is South Africa, for such illusory 'Bantustans'.

Commenting on a suggestion by Professor du Plessis that a federation of 'Bantustans' be established, Mr Duma Nokwe, secretary-general of the African National Congress, totally rejected such a plan as unacceptable. The correct approach, he said, would be the extension of the franchise rights to Africans. Thereafter a National Convention of all the people of South Africa could be summoned and numerous suggestions of the democratic changes that should be brought about, including the suggestion of Professor du Plessis, could form the subject of the Convention.

Here, indeed, Mr Nokwe has put his finger on the spot. There is no need for Dr Eiselen, Mrs Ballinger, or others to argue about 'what the Africans think' about the future of this country. Let the people speak for themselves! Let us have a free vote and a free election of delegates to a national convention, irrespective of colour or nationality. Let the Nationalists submit their plan, and the Congress its Charter. If Verwoerd and Eiselen think the Africans support their schemes they need not fear such a procedure. If they are not prepared to submit to public opinion, then let them stop parading and pretending to the outside world that they are democrats, and talking revolting nonsense about 'Bantu self-government'.

Dr Verwoerd may deceive the simple-minded Nationalist voters with his talk of Bantustans, but he will not deceive anyone else, neither the African people, nor the great world beyond the borders of this country. We have heard such talk before, and we know what it means. Like everything else that has come from the Nationalist Government, it spells nothing but fresh hardships and suffering to the masses of the people.

Behind the fine talk of 'self-government' is a sinister design.

The abolition of African representation in Parliament and the Cape Provincial Council shows that the real purpose of the scheme is not to concede autonomy to Africans but to deprive them of all say in the government of the country in exchange for a system of local government controlled by a minister who is not responsible to them but to a Parliament in which they have no voice. This is not autonomy but autocracy.

Contact between the minister and the Bantu authorities will be maintained by five commissioners-general. These officials will act as the watchdogs of the minister to ensure that the 'authorities' strictly toe the line. Their duty will be to ensure that these authorities should not become the voice of the African people but that of the Nationalist Government.

In terms of the White Paper, steps will be taken to 'link' Africans working in urban areas with the territorial authorities established under the Bantu Authorities Act by conferring powers on these authorities to nominate persons as their representatives in urban areas. This means in effect that efforts will be made to place Africans in the cities under the control of their tribal chiefs—a retrograde step.

Nowhere in the Bill or in the various proclamations dealing with the creation of Bantu authorities is there provision for democratic elections by Africans falling within the jurisdiction of the authorities.

In the light of these facts it is sheer nonsense to talk of South Africa as being about to take a 'supremely positive step towards placing Africans on the road to self-government', or of having given them more powers to rule themselves. As Dr Eiselen clearly pointed out in his article in *Optima*, the establishment of Bantu-

stans will not in any way affect White supremacy since even in
such areas Whites will stay supreme. The Bantustans are not
intended to voice aspirations of the African people; they are
instruments for their subjection. Under the pretext of giving them
self-government the African people are being split up into tribal
units in order to retard their growth and development into full
nationhood.

The new Bantu Bill and the policy behind it will bear heavily
on the peasants in the Reserves. But it is not they who are the
chief target of Verwoerd's new policy.

His new measures are aimed, in the first place, at the millions
of Africans in the great cities of this country, the factory workers
and intellectuals who have raised the banner of freedom and
democracy and human dignity, who have spoken forth boldly the
message that is shaking imperialism to its foundations throughout
this great continent of Africa.

The Nationalists hate and fear that banner and that message.
They will try to destroy them, by striking with all their might at
the standard-bearer and vanguard of the people, the working class.

Behind the 'self-government' talks lies a grim programme of
mass evictions, political persecution, and police terror. It is the
last desperate gamble of a hated and doomed fascist autocracy—
which, fortunately, is soon due to make its exit from the stage of
history.

May 1959

9

THE Treason Trial began twenty days before Christmas in 1956 with a mass police swoop and the arrest of 156 political leaders of all races. They were guilty, charged the State, of a treasonable conspiracy inspired by international communism to overthrow the South African State by violence. A preparatory examination forecast by the Prosecutor to last six weeks lasted ten months. The trial itself went on for over four years. Some of the accused were discharged at the end of the first year; the fate of others hung on the outcome of the trial of the first twenty-nine. Mandela was among these. The focus of the State case was African National Congress policy from 1952 to 1956 and every document written by or in the possession of every accused was studied minutely. The State case was eventually narrowed down to an attempt to prove the intention of the accused to act violently.

Day after day, week after week, year after year, Mandela sat in the dock all day and in his law office till late at night. The trial was a test of endurance. The offence of treason is punishable by the death sentence and the accused in the dock had this prospect confronting them. Nevertheless, their daily political activity went on.

In 1959 the Treason Trial was not yet over, but the Congress was organizing an anti-pass campaign. 1960 was to be Africa Year and in South Africa it was to be anti-pass year. Events were snatched from the grasp of Congress when the Pan-Africanist Congress, which had split away on a policy dispute, called for mass anti-pass protests on 21 March. The police opened fire in two centres: in the Sharpeville massacre sixty-nine were killed and 180 wounded, and at Langa two were killed and forty-nine wounded. The ANC called for a strike as a national day of mourning. The Government wavered, for a moment, with its announcement that pass laws would be suspended. Chief Lutuli publicly burnt his pass, followed by thousands of others. It looked as though the people held the initiative. Then a state of national emergency was declared, and the African National Congress was banned, together with PAC.

Eighteen hundred politicals were imprisoned, among them Mandela and the other accused in the Treason Trial who had been on bail.

The ANC was illegal and it was a serious offence to carry on its activities and advocate its aims, but within a fortnight of the banning order a caretaker committee had been formed and leaflets attacking the pass laws were circulating in the African townships.

The team of defence lawyers withdrew from the Treason Trial. It was impossible to conduct a defence in a political trial in a time of stringent emergency, they declared. The accused conducted their own defence. Mandela was elected spokesman of the prisoners in Pretoria jail and he, Walter Sisulu, Duma Nokwe, Robert Resha, and Ahmed Kathrada prepared their case and led their fellow-accused in evidence.

Four hundred pages of the official Treason Trial record is taken up by the evidence-in-chief and the cross-examination of Mandela. Much of the State's cross-examination was of speeches and articles by him, prominent among them the presidential address 'No Easy Walk to Freedom'. He was questioned on his attitude to violence and non-violence, and his view of the Freedom Charter.

The extracts below are some of the statements he made:

A CHARGE OF TREASON

On the Document called 'Basic Policy of the ANCYL'

COUNSEL FOR THE DEFENCE: What was the aim of the ANC with regard to Nationalism on the one hand and tribes on the other hand?—It was always the policy of the ANC to bring about out of the various African tribal groups in the country a united African community.

As far as the Union of South Africa was concerned, did you regard it as a country which was subject to foreign domination?—We regarded it as subject to White supremacy.

Apart from the question of organization, did the Youth League feel that the methods and activity used by the ANC should be changed?—Up to the time that the Youth League was formed and until 1949 the only methods of political action which were adopted by the ANC were purely constitutional: deputations to see the authorities, memoranda, and the mere passing of resolutions. We felt that that policy had been tried out and found wanting and we thought that the ANC, its organizers and field workers, should go out into the highways and organize the masses of the African people for mass campaigns. We felt that the time had arrived for the Congress to consider the adoption of more militant forms of political action: stay-at-homes, civil disobedience, protests, demonstrations—also including the methods which had previously been employed by the ANC.

On Communists

Were some members of the Youth League actually in favour of expelling Communists from the ANC?—Yes, my Lords. As a matter of fact the Youth League moved a resolution at conferences of the ANC calling on the ANC to expel Communists, but these resolutions were defeated by an overwhelming majority.

On what grounds were these resolutions rejected?—The view of the ANC was that every person above the age of seventeen years irrespective of the political views he might have was entitled to become a member of the ANC.

What was your own view at the time?—At that time I strongly supported the resolution to expel the Communists from the ANC . . .

(Mandela then indicated that from about 1960 he had for the first time worked with Communists in the ANC.)

Whatever may have been their opinions or intentions, as far as you were concerned did it appear to you that they were followers of ANC policy?—That is correct.

Did they appear loyal to it?—That is correct.

Did you become a Communist?—Well, I don't know if I did become a Communist. If by Communist you mean a member of the Communist Party and a person who believes in the theory of Marx, Engels, Lenin, and Stalin, and who adheres strictly to the discipline of the party, I did not become a Communist.

On the 1949 Programme of Action

How did you understand the new Programme of Action?—My Lord, up to 1949 the leaders of the ANC had always acted in the hope that by merely pleading their cause, placing it before the authorities, they, the authorities, would change their hearts and extend to them all the rights that they were demanding. But the forms of political action which are set out in the Programme of

Action meant that the ANC was not going to rely on a change of heart. It was going to exert pressure to compel the authorities to grant its demands.

On the Suppression of Communism Act

. . . Well, in regard to the Act, the ANC took the view that the Act was an invasion of the rights of our political organizations, that it was not only aimed against the Communist Party of South Africa, but was designed to attack and destroy all the political organizations that condemned the racialist policies of the South African Government. We felt that even if it were aimed against the Communist Party of South Africa we would still oppose it, because we believe that every political organization has a right to exist and to advocate its own point of view.

On the Defiance Campaign

Do you think that, apart from the increase in your membership, it (the Defiance Campaign) had any other result?—Yes, most certainly. Firstly, it pricked the conscience of the European public which became aware in a much more clear manner of the sufferings and disabilities of the African people. It led directly to the formation of the Congress of Democrats. It also influenced the formation of the Liberal Party. It also led to discussions on the policies of apartheid at the United Nations and I think to that extent it was an outstanding success.

Do you think it had any effect at all on the Government?—I think it had. After the Defiance Campaign the Government began talking about self-government for Africans, Bantustans. I do not believe, of course, that the Government was in any way sincere in saying it was part of Government policy to extend autonomy to Africans. I think they acted in order to deceive . . . but in spite of that deception one thing comes out very clearly and that is that they acknowledged the power of the Defiance Campaign, they felt the striking power of the ANC had tremendously increased . . .

MR JUSTICE BEKKER: Well, as a matter of fact, isn't your freedom a direct threat to the Europeans?—No, it is not a direct threat to the Europeans. We are not anti-White, we are against White supremacy and in struggling against White supremacy we have the support of some sections of the European population and we have made this clear from time to time. As a matter of fact, in the letter we wrote to the then Prime Minister of the country, Dr Malan, before we launched the Defiance Campaign, we said that the campaign we were about to launch was not directed against any racial group. It was a campaign which was directed against laws which we considered unjust, and time without number the ANC has explained this . . . It is quite clear that the Congress has consistently preached a policy of race harmony and we have condemned racialism no matter by whom it is professed.

On the One-party System

My Lord, it is not a question of form, it is a question of democracy. If democracy would be best expressed by a one-party system I would examine the proposition very carefully. But if democracy could best be expressed by a multi-party system then I would examine that carefully. In this country, for example, we have a multi-party system at present, but so far as the non-Europeans are concerned this is the most vicious despotism you could think of.

On a Classless Society

Are you attracted by the idea of a classless society?—Yes, very much so, my Lord. I think that a lot of evils arise out of the existence of classes, one class exploiting others (but) . . . the ANC has no policy in any shape or form on this matter.

On the Liberal Party

Do you adhere today to the attitude you then expressed towards the Liberal Party?—I still do except that the Liberal Party has now shifted a great deal from its original position. It is now working more closely with the Congress movement and to a very large extent it has accepted a great portion of the policy of the Congress movement. I also believe that in regard to the question of the qualified vote there has been some healthy development of outlook which brings it still closer to our policy. To that extent some of the views I expressed in that article have now been qualified.

Imperialism

In our experience the most important thing about imperialism today is that it has gone all over the world subjugating people and exploiting them, bringing death and destruction to millions of people. That is the central thing and we want to know whether we should support and perpetuate this institution which has brought so much suffering.

1960

RESISTANCE FROM
UNDERGROUND

10

Editor's note

AFTER a trial lasting four and a half years in which the lives of the accused had been disrupted and the organization of Congress sorely strained, verdict was delivered in the Treason Trial. Mr Justice Rumpff pronounced: 'You are found not guilty and discharged. You may go.'

Alfred Hutchinson, writer and himself one of the accused, wrote: 'What treason was there? Is it treason to ask that Black and White should live together, as brothers, countrymen, equals? Is it treason to ask for food? Is it treason to ask that passes be abolished? And that we might walk freely in the land of our birth?'*

The trial was over, but so were the legal days of the African National Congress. Next steps had to be decided.

'It was during the long years of the Treason Trial that onlookers began to take notice of Mandela,' Mary Benson wrote. 'It was not only that he, with Duma Nokwe, distinguished himself when the defence team withdrew during the 1960 Emergency and left the defence in their hands during those tense months. It was not just the articulate attack of his evidence and the political intelligence this showed; it was something much deeper. It was a question of growth, and all sorts of people quite apart from friends or supporters of the freedom movement suddenly became aware of it and began to refer to "Mandela's increasing stature". So it was that in 1960, when the ANC had been outlawed . . . and it seemed that the movement for liberation must surely be numbed by the long imprisonments of the Emergency, that the time was ripe for a fresh lead, and a man was ripe for the moment.'

The African National Congress and the Pan-Africanist Congress were banned but the country was in a state of ferment. An *ad-hoc* committee of African leaders, among them the Reverend Rajuili, Paul Mosaka, W. B. Ngakane, Duma Nokwe, Julius Mali, Govan Mbeki, Joe Molefe, the Reverend N. B. Tantsi, Alfred Nzo, C. Mbata, Marks Shope, and J. Ngubane, summoned an All-In African Conference in Pietermaritzburg for March 1961.

* In the South African monthly, *Fighting Talk*, now banned—*Ed.*

White South Africa was preparing a referendum to declare itself a Nationalist Republic; the freedom struggle urged that there was one last opportunity to prevent race disaster. There should be convened a full representative gathering—representative of all races—a new national convention to draft a new, democratic constitution. The disfranchised were determined to assert their claim to participate in government.

Mandela had been banned from gatherings for nine years, and the last set of bans was due to expire on the eve of the conference. Anticipating a renewal of the restrictions and impending widespread arrests of leaders he went into hiding . . . and then suddenly appeared at the conference to deliver the keynote speech. The effect on the delegates drawn from village and factory from many parts of the country, with impressive representation from the traditional areas of Zululand, Pondoland, and the Transkei, was electric. Mandela was elected leader of the National Action Council which was charged by the conference with the campaign for a National Convention and, if that were ignored by the Government, with a strike and a campaign of non-cooperation.

Mandela's natural authority and dedication were to inspire the campaign throughout. No sooner were the conference proceedings over than he was announcing its message and meaning to the country.

THE STRUGGLE FOR A NATIONAL CONVENTION

'I AM attending this conference as delegate from my village. I was elected at a secret meeting held in the bushes far away from our kraals simply because in our village it is now a crime for us to hold meetings. I have listened most carefully to speeches made here and they have given me strength and courage. I now realize that we are not alone. But I am troubled by my experiences during the last weeks. In the course of our struggle against the system of Bantu Authorities,* we heard many fighting speeches delivered by men we trusted most, but when the hour of decision came they did not have the courage of their convictions. They deserted us and we felt lonely and without friends. But I will go away from here refreshed and full of confidence. We must win in the end.'

* Government puppet local Councils—*Ed.*

These words were said at the All-In African Conference held at Pietermaritzburg on 25 and 26 March. The man who said them came from a country area where the people are waging a consistent struggle against Bantu authorities. He wore riding breeches, a khaki shirt, an old jacket, and came to conference bare-footed. But his words held fire and dignity and his remarks, like those of other speakers, indicated that this conference was no talking shop for persons who merely wanted to let off steam, but a solemn gathering which appreciated the grave decisions it was called upon to take.

The theme of the conference was African unity and the calling, by the Government, of a national convention of elected representatives of all adult men and women, on an equal basis, irrespective of race, colour or creed, with full powers to determine a new democratic constitution for South Africa.

Conference resolved that if the Government failed to call this convention by 31 May, country-wide demonstrations would be held on the eve of the Republic in protest against this undemocratic act.

The adoption of this part of the resolution did not mean that conference preferred a monarchy to a republican form of government. Such considerations were unimportant and irrelevant. The point at issue, and which was emphasized over and over again by delegates, was that a minority Government had decided to proclaim a White Republic under which the living conditions of the African people would continue to deteriorate.

Conference further resolved that, in the event of the Government failing to accede to this demand, all Africans would be called upon not to cooperate with the proposed Republic. All sections of our population would be asked to unite with us in opposing the Nationalists.

The resolution went further and called upon democratic people the world over to impose economic and other sanctions against the Government. A National Action Council was elected to implement the above decisions.

Three other resolutions were passed in which the arrest of members of the Continuation Committee was strongly condemned; and in which conference called for the lifting of the ban imposed on the African National Congress and the Pan-Africanist Congress. The system of Bantu Authorities was attacked as a measure forcibly imposed by the Government in spite of the unanimous opposition of the entire African nation.

These resolutions were adopted unanimously by more than 1,500 delegates, from town and country, representing 150 political, religious, sporting, and cultural organizations.

Members of the Liberal Party, the Inter-Denominational African Ministers' Federation, the Eastwood Advisory Board, the Zenzele Club, and scores of other organizations from all over the country, spoke with one voice and jointly faced the political changes thrown out by the Nationalist Government.

For thirteen hours they earnestly and calmly considered the grave political situation that has risen in South Africa as a result of the disastrous policies of the present régime.

Now and again, discussions were interrupted by stirring tunes sung with intense feeling and tremendous enthusiasm by the entire conference. The favourite song was 'Amandla Ngawethu' composed by the freedom fighters of Port Elizabeth during the recent bus boycott in that city.

The gathering was a moving demonstration of the comradeship and solidarity and was acclaimed by the South African Press as an outstanding success.

The main resolution showed that the delegates visualized much more than a token demonstration on the chosen dates. The people contemplated a stubborn and prolonged struggle, involving masses of the people from town and country, and taking different forms in accordance with local conditions, beginning before 31 May and which would continue unabated until democratic reforms are instituted.

Delegates fully appreciated that the above decisions were not directed against any other population group in the country. They were aimed at a form of government based on brute force and condemned the world over as inhuman and dangerous. It was precisely because of this fact that Conference called on the Coloured and Indian people and all European democrats to join forces with us.

It will indeed be very tragic if, in the momentous days that lie ahead, White South Africa will falter and adopt a course of action which will prevent the successful implementation of the resolutions of conference.

In the past we have been astonished by the reaction of certain political parties and 'philanthropic' associations which proclaimed themselves to be anti-apartheid but which, nevertheless, consistently opposed positive action taken by the oppressed people to defeat this same policy. Objectively, such an attitude can only serve to defend White domination and to strengthen the Nationalist Party. It also serves to weaken the impact of liberal views amongst European democrats and lays them open to the charge of being hypocritical.

All the democratic forces in this country must join in a programme of democratic changes. If they are not prepared to come along with us, they can at least be neutral and leave this Government isolated and without friends.

Finally, however successful the conference was from the point of view of attendance and the fiery nature of the speeches made, these militant resolutions will remain useless and ineffective unless we translate them into practice.

If we form local action committees in our respective areas, popularize the decisions through vigorous and systematic house-to-house campaigns, we will inspire and arouse the country to implement the resolutions and to hasten the fall of the Nationalist Government within our lifetime.

March 1961

II

Editor's note

THE demand for the holding of a national convention to draft a new, non-colour-bar constitution, was the claim of the disfranchised, the overwhelming majority of South Africans, that the vote be extended to them. The stay-at-home that followed the Pietermaritzburg conference was a dramatic action to drive this demand home.

The Government answered the strike call with the country's biggest mobilization since the war. Army and police staged an unprecedented display of armed force. Civil liberties were suspended. The whole armoury of intimidation and coercion was brought into play. Men and women were arrested and held without trial on the suspicion that they might be working to organize the strike. Printers' premises were raided and all printed publicity for the strike was seized. Mandela organized from hiding, joining issue with the Press on their handling of the strike, signing personal appeals to youth leaders and sportsmen, directing a special propaganda campaign into the schools and colleges, paying surprise visits to key industrial areas. Immediately after the strike he wrote a detailed analysis of it, and this long article was published by the underground ANC offices in South Africa and by its offices abroad.

GENERAL STRIKE

THE call of the All-In African National Action Council* for a stay-at-home on 29, 30, and 31 May 1961 received solid and massive support throughout the country. This magnificent response was the result of the hard work and selfless devotion of our organizers and activists who had to overcome formidable difficulties very often involving personal risks to themselves. Defying unprecedented intimidation by the State, trailed and hounded by the Special Branch, denied the right to hold meetings,

* Later referred to in this article as the NAC—*Ed.*

operating in areas heavily patrolled by Government and municipal police and teeming with spies and informers, they stood firm as a rock and spread the stay-at-home message to millions of people throughout the country. Ever since the All-In African Conference at Pietermaritzburg, the issue that dominated South African politics and that attracted Pressmen from all over the world was not the Republication celebrations organized by the Government, but the stirring campaign of the African people and other non-White sections to mark our rejection of a White Republic forcibly imposed upon us by a minority.

Few political organizations could have succeeded in conducting such a stubborn and relentless campaign under conditions which, for all practical purposes, amounted to martial law. But we did so. The steps taken by the Government to suppress the campaign were a measure of our strength and influence in the political life of the country and of its weakness. The Government was alarmed by the tremendous impact of the demand for a national convention and the call for country-wide anti-Republican demonstrations. It realized that there would be overwhelming support for the call if the campaign was not immediately suppressed through open terror and intimidation. It also realized that the organizational machine built up to propagate the campaign was of so high a standard, and support for the idea so firm and widespread, that the situation could only be controlled by resorting to naked force. Only by mobilizing the entire resources of the State could the Government hope to stem the tide that was running so strongly against it.

A special law had to be rushed through Parliament to enable the Government to detain without trial people connected with the organization of the stay-at-home. The Army had to be called out, European civilians armed, and the police force deployed in African townships and other areas. Meetings were banned throughout the country, and the local authorities, in collaboration with the police force, kept vigil to ensure that no strike propaganda should be spread amongst the masses of the people. More than 10,000 innocent Africans were arrested and jailed under the pass laws and terror and intimidation became widespread. Only by adopting these strong-arm measures could the Government hope to break the stay-at-home. By resorting to these drastic steps the

Government has in fact conceded that we are the country's most powerful and dangerous opponents to its hated policies.

On this issue, the radio, the Press, and European employers played a thoroughly shameful role. At the beginning of the campaign the Press gave us a fairly objective coverage and, acting on information supplied by their own reporters in different parts of the country, they reported growing support for the demonstrations and correctly predicted unprecedented response to the call. Until a week or so before the stay-at-home, the South African Press endeavoured to live up to the standards and ethics of honest journalism and reported news items as they were without slants and distortions. But as soon as the Government showed the mailed fist and threatened action against those newspapers that gave publicity to the campaign, the Opposition Press, true to tradition, beat a hurried retreat and threw all principles and ethical standards overboard. . . .

Undue prominence was given to statements made by Government leaders, mayors of cities, managers of non-European Affairs departments, and by employers' organizations, in which the stay-at-home was condemned and appeals made to workers to ignore the call. Statements made by the NAC were either distorted, watered down, or even suppressed deliberately. For example, on 20 May 1961 the NAC issued a Press statement strongly protesting at the unwarranted arrest of more than 10,000 innocent Africans. We condemned this police action as a blatant persecution of our voteless people by a European minority which we could no longer tolerate. We placed on record that we were deeply incensed by this provocative action and demanded the immediate stopping of the arrests and the unconditional release of all those detained. Not a single Opposition newspaper published this statement notwithstanding the extensive publicity they gave this police operation and the unwarranted compliment they paid to the same police for the courteous manner in which they were alleged to have carried out the operation. These arrests were made for the purpose of forestalling demonstrations planned by us. We had gone through numerous road blocks in various parts of the country and it was our people who had been rounded up under a system which is rejected by the entire African nation and which has been condemned by every Government Commission which considered it. Was it not important for the country to know what our views were on a matter of such importance?

The Press was even more treacherous on the morning of the first day of the stay-at-home. The deliberate falsehoods spread by the police and radio were reproduced. At seven o'clock in the morning of that day, Radio South Africa broadcast news that workers throughout the country had ignored the call for a stay-at-home. The country was told that this news was based on statements made at six o'clock the same morning by Col. Spengler, head of the Witwatersrand branch of the Special Branch. Similar statements made at approximately the same time by other police officers in different parts of the country were quoted.* This means that long before the factory gates were opened and, in some areas, even before the workers boarded their trains and buses to work, the police had already announced that the stay-at-home had collapsed. I cannot imagine anything more fraudulent.

But the truth could not be suppressed for long. The Johannesburg *Star* of the same day reported that 'Early estimates of absenteeism in Johannesburg ranged from 40 per cent to 75 per cent'. This admission was only a small portion of the truth. As the days rolled by, news came through that hundreds of thousands of workers and students throughout the country had given massive support to the call. On 3 June 1961, *Post*, a Johannesburg Sunday newspaper with a huge circulation, published reports from its team of crack reporters and photographers who had kept a continuous watch on townships in different parts of South Africa and who conducted detailed personal investigations inside and outside of these areas. Said the newspaper: 'Many thousands of workers registered their protest against the Republic and the Government's refusal to cooperate with non-Whites. THEY DID NOT GO TO WORK. They disrupted much of South African commerce and industry. Some factories worked with skeleton staffs, others closed, and many other businesses were shut down for the three days.' The leading article of the *New Age*

---

* In the trial of Nokwe and others arising out of the Pietermaritzburg conference, the State led evidence to prove the opposite: that 'incitement' had provoked a successful strike. The manager of a bus company said 75 per cent of Johannesburg workers carried on his transport system had been on strike—*Ed.*

of 8 June 1961 acclaimed the stay-at-home as the most widespread
general strike on a national scale that this country had ever seen.

Contact of 1 June 1961 wrote: 'On Tuesday 50 per cent of
Indian workers in Durban were still out. Some factories showed
100 per cent success with some clothing factories 100 per cent
unattended. In Durban and Pietermaritzburg most Indian
businesses were closed on Monday and open again on Tuesday.
Large numbers of schoolchildren kept away from school. There
were attacks on buses at Cato Manor and a bus to Pietermaritzburg
from a Reserve was fired on.' Sam Sly, writing in the same paper
on 15 June 1961, observed: 'In defiance of that sickening and
sterile rule, there were plenty of politics on plenty of campuses.
Enough to bring large bands of armed police to five campuses.
There was defiance, leadership, and courage amongst the students.
There was political awareness, even non-racial solidarity. Before,
what had one heard but minority protests lost among the sounds
of the inter-varsity rugby crowd or the chatter in the students'
cafeteria.'

A Port Elizabeth daily newspaper estimated that about 75 per
cent of that city's non-White population stayed away on 30 May
1961.

The truth had come out. From various parts of the country
news came through testifying to widespread support for the
call.

Students at the University College of Fort Hare, at Healdtown
and Lovedale all stayed away from classes. At the University of
Natal, which has about 500 non-White students, less than fifty
attended classes. Throughout the country thousands of students
in primary and secondary schools stayed away from classes and
boycotted Republican celebrations. The Transkeian Territories
have been under martial law for many months now. The bar-
barous and cruel policies of the Nationalist Government find
expression in extremely savage attacks on the innocent and unarmed people of these areas. Many have been murdered by the
Government and their stooges, thousands have been beaten up
and injured, uprooted and driven away from their lands and
homes. Hundreds of freedom fighters are languishing in jails for
demanding freedom and justice for the people of the Transkei.
Even in this area of death and hell, the flames of freedom are

scorching meadows. Umtata, the capital of the area, bore witness to this fact the other day. Students of St John's College, in a militant and inspiring demonstration, showed that the days of despots and tyrants are numbered.

A detailed survey conducted by the South African Congress of Trade Unions shows that in Johannesburg, Durban, Port Elizabeth, Cape Town and other centres, the clothing, textile, laundry and dry-cleaning, food and canning, and the furniture industries were severely hit.

In the light of the conditions that prevailed both before and during the three-day strike, the response from our people was magnificent indeed. The failure of the Government, the employers, and the Press to break us down pays tribute to the matchless courage and determination of our people and to the skilful and speedy manner in which our organizational machine was able to adapt itself to new conditions, new obstacles, new dangers. . . .

The attitude of former members of the Pan-Africanist Congress on the stay-at-home has been one of shocking contradiction and amazing confusion. Nothing has been more disastrous to themselves than their pathetic attempts to sabotage the demonstrations.

First, they attended the Consultative Conference of African leaders held in Orlando in December 1960 as delegates, took part in the deliberations and fully supported the resolution adopted at that conference calling for unity amongst Africans and for a multi-racial national convention. At this conference a Continuation Committee was elected to prepare for the All-In African Conference which was subsequently held at Pietermaritzburg. Their representative served on this committee for several months with full knowledge that its main function was to unite all Africans on an anti-Republic front and for a sovereign convention of all South Africans to draw up a new democratic constitution for the country. Towards the end of February this year, and without so much as a hint to their colleagues on the Continuation Committee, they issued a Press statement announcing that they would not take part in the Pietermaritzburg talks. Their failure to raise the matter in the committee before they withdrew betrays the underhand and traitorous nature of this manoeuvre and indicates that they well knew that they could find no political justification whatsoever for their action.

Secondly, there was a sharp conflict between former leaders of the PAC on the South African United Front overseas and the local leaders. Whilst the latter opposed, the former gave support. A message from Dar-es-Salaam, signed by J. J. Hadebe and Gaur Radebe, former members of the ANC and PAC respectively, said:

'The South African United Front congratulates the Continuation Committee of the people's conference held at Pietermaritzburg for organizing demonstrations on the eve of the South African Republic which threatens to further oppress and persecute the people.'

Even locally there were many former PAC people who bitterly disagreed with their leaders and who felt that they could not follow the stupid and disastrous blunders they were advocating.

But there was something even more disastrous and tragic than their mean and cowardly behaviour in stabbing their kith and kin at a time when maximum unity had become a matter of life and death to Africans. What shocked most people was the extent to which they completely identified themselves with the action of the police in the repression of the demonstrations. We have already indicated the unprecedented measures adopted by the Government to deal with our campaign. These measures provoked strong protests from many organizations and individuals, but there was not a single word of protest from the former PAC people. Why? Precisely because their main function was to ruin African unity and to break the strike. To protest against these savage onslaughts on the African people would have been an unfriendly act to the Government with whom they were now allied. They purchased collaboration with the Government at the price of turning a deaf ear to the sufferings of the African people. At the hour of crisis, they were on the side of the Government, helping to crush the struggle of the oppressed people.

Authentic reports from different parts of the country revealed that the police did not interfere with the distribution of PAC leaflets and, in some areas, members of the police force even distributed leaflets purporting to have been issued by the PAC and attacking the strike.

This collaboration was not confined to negative acts of passivity. In its positive form it expressed itself in desperate attempts both by the police and the PAC people to track down the people behind the campaign. For security reasons, the identity of members of the NAC was kept a closely guarded secret. The police conducted extensive investigations to find this information in order to arrest members of this body. At the same time the PAC people called on us to publish the information and protested that we had to communicate with the Press from public telephone booths. Why were they interested in this information? They knew all the members of the Continuation Committee. They withdrew from that committee and from the campaign not because they did not know its members but in spite of that knowledge. Such information was useless to them because they were out of the campaign but extremely useful to the police. On which side of the fence are these people? What sort of political organization is this that deliberately sets traps for leaders of another political body? Who are they trying to bluff by pretending that they are still against the Government and fighting for the welfare of the African people?

Differences between rival political organizations in the liberation camp on tactical questions are permissible. But for a political body which purports to be part of the liberation struggle to pursue a line which objectively supports a Government that suppresses Africans is treacherous and unforgivable. We called on the African people to reject the Verwoerd Republic not because we preferred a monarchical form of government, but because we felt that the introduction of a Republic should only take place after seeking the views and after obtaining the express consent of the African people. We felt that the foundations of the Republic, as of the State that existed prior to the proclamation of the Republic, would be based on apartheid and the exploitation of the African people. The Government rejected our demands, called upon the African people to ignore our call and to participate fully in the Republican celebrations and to cooperate with the new Government. The Africanists echoed the Government by asking Africans to ignore the call but deliberately elected to remain silent on the vital question whether or not they should cooperate with the Republic. An ingenious way of saying that we should participate and cooperate.

A political organization that is forced by opportunism and petty political rivalries into allying itself with the enemies of an oppressed community is doomed. The African people demand freedom and self-rule. They refuse to cooperate with the Verwoerd Republic or with any Government based upon force. PAC has ruined its future by opposing this dynamic demand. That is why most Africans, including many who once supported them, are so strong in condemning their treachery.

But all this discussion has now become academic because for all practical purposes PAC has lost considerable support even in areas where only last year it achieved spectacular success. In February this year they announced plans to stage demonstrations from 21 March 1961. Leaflets were issued in Cape Town and were widely distributed in Langa and Nyanga African townships calling upon people to stock food and to prepare themselves for action on this date. In Johannesburg and Vereeniging stickers appeared here and there calling upon Africans to observe 21 March as the day of struggle. The whole thing fizzled out long before the much-heralded day, and when the date arrived not a single person responded either in Cape Town, Vereeniging, or Johannesburg. The episode was not regarded as sufficiently newsworthy even to be mentioned as a failure by the Press either here or abroad. For the second time in two months they have suffered yet another defeat. Their efforts to sabotage the recent strike misfired badly. Hundreds of thousands of workers throughout the country, businessmen in town and country and thousands upon thousands of students in primary and secondary schools, treated the PAC with utter contempt and responded magnificently to our call. The results prove that no power on earth can stop an oppressed population determined to win its freedom. In the meantime, PAC has been shocked and stunned by this rebuff and they sit licking their wounds, unable to look people in the face and haunted by the enormity of their outrageous crime.

One of the most significant factors about the stay-at-home was the wide support it received from students and the militant and stirring demonstrations it inspired amongst them. African students at Fort Hare, Natal University, Lovedale, Healdtown and in many other primary and secondary schools throughout the country demonstrated their support for the call and stayed away from lectures. In primary and secondary schools throughout the country, scholars boycotted Republican celebrations, refused commemoration medals, and stayed away from schools. There were militant and inspiring demonstrations at St John's College at Umtata and at the Botha Sigcawu College in the Transkei. There were equally impressive ones in Kilnerton and Bloemfontein. This is an extremely significant development because students are the life-blood of a political movement and the upsurge of national consciousness amongst them spells death and destruction to those who oppose the claims and legitimate aspirations of the African people.

European students at the University of Rhodes, at the Witwatersrand University, also played a prominent part in the demonstrations. Their support showed that even amongst the Whites the forces of challenge and opposition to White supremacy exist and are ready to join battle whenever the call is made.

On 1 June 1961, the NAC issued a Press statement strongly condemning the victimization of students who participated in the strike and demanded that the tyrannical orders for the closing of some of the colleges should be withdrawn and the colleges reopened at once. We congratulated the students for their public-spirited action in which, as befits the intellectual youth, they gave a courageous lead to the nation at a time when courage and leadership were qualities we needed most. However much the authorities may try to play down the importance and significance of this development amongst the African youth, there can be no doubt that they realize that the writing is on the wall and that the days of White supremacy in our country are numbered.

The response of the Coloured people was equally impressive. They showed immense courage and militancy. In a country where they have always been treated as an appendage of the ruling White group and in which official policy had tended to treat them differently from the rest of the non-White population, it is significant and most heartening that they decided to make common cause with us by coming clearly against the Verwoerd Republic. This development marks a landmark in the political struggles of the non-Whites in this country.

The entire Indian community threw its powerful resources behind the campaign. Indian workers stayed away from work. Businessmen closed their businesses and students stayed away from schools and refused medals.

The forces of liberation are strong and powerful and their

numbers are growing. The morale is high and we look forward to the future with perfect confidence.

It would, however, be a mistake to exaggerate our success. In spite of the magnificent courage shown by our people, numerical response fell below expectations. Mistakes were committed and weaknesses and shortcomings were discovered. They must be attended to. We must make adjustments in our methods and style of work to meet contingencies which we did not anticipate. Only in this way shall we build more strength and increase our striking power.

People expressed the view that the issue on which the people were asked to strike, namely, the demand for a national convention, lacked emotional appeal and was, in any event, too complicated an issue to arouse enthusiasm. Facts contradict this viewpoint. The success of the Pietermaritzburg conference and the deep and widespread support for the eve of the Republic demonstrations testified to not only by our organizers and activists, but by the South African Press, and the fact that hundreds of thousands of people stayed away from work notwithstanding fierce intimidation by the Government and threats of dismissal by employers, indicate that this issue aroused the greatest enthusiasm. What reduced the scope and extent of what would have been an unprecedented response were the drastic measures taken by the Government to suppress the strike, intimidation by employers, and the falsehoods spread by the radio and the Press.

A closely related argument is that the demand for a National convention does not deal with bread-and-butter issues. Of course the African people want bread and butter. Is there anybody who does not? We demand higher wages and we want more and better food in our pantries. But we also need the vote to legislate decent laws. This is the importance of the demand for a national convention. One man one vote is the key to our future.

Another argument is that the strike was called by an *ad hoc* committee whose members were unknown to the public, that the voice of Chief A. J. Lutuli, the most powerful and popular leader of the African people, and that of the African National Congress, the sword and shield of the African people for the last fifty years, were never heard. The argument continues that the public may have doubted whether the African leaders were in fact behind the demonstration. In the first place, Chief Lutuli was a member of the Continuation Committee which organized the Pietermaritzburg conference and he sent a dynamic message to that gathering which was loudly cheered. In the second place, the names of members of the NAC were, for obvious reasons, never published and the public may never know whether or not Chief Lutuli was a member. It would have been naïve for us to have stood on the mountain tops and proclaimed that he was a member directing his forces as he has always done in previous campaigns. His courage and devotion to the cause of freedom is known in every household in this country. Inside and outside committees he remains the undisputed and most respected leader of the African people and a source of tremendous inspiration to all South African freedom fighters. He is a fearless opponent of the Nationalist Government and leader of all the anti-Republican forces.

Of all the observations made on the strike, none has brought forth so much heat and emotion as the stress and emphasis we put on non-violence. Our most loyal supporters, whose courage and devotion has never been doubted, unanimously and strenuously disagreed with this approach and with the assurances we gave that we would not use any form of intimidation whatsoever to induce people to stay away from work. It was argued that the soil of our beloved country has been stained with the priceless blood of African patriots murdered by the Nationalist Government in the course of peaceful and disciplined demonstrations to assert their claims and legitimate aspirations. It was the Government that should have been told to refrain from its inhuman policy of violence and massacre, not the African people. It was further argued that it is wrong and indefensible for a political organization to repudiate picketing, which is used the world over as a legitimate form of pressure to prevent scabbing.

Even up to the present day the question that is being asked with monotonous regularity up and down the country is this: Is it politically correct to continue preaching peace and non-violence when dealing with a Government whose barbaric practices have brought so much suffering and misery to Africans? With equal monotony the question is posed: Have we not closed a chapter on this question? These are crucial questions that merit sane and

sober reflection. It would be a serious mistake to brush them aside
and leave them unanswered.

The strike at the end of May was only the beginning of our
campaign. We are now launching a full-scale, country-wide
campaign of non-cooperation with the Verwoerd Government,
until we have won an elected National Convention, representing
all the people of this country, with the power to draw up and
enforce a new democratic constitution.

Details of the campaign will be given from time to time. But
let me say now that people without votes cannot be expected to
go on paying taxes to a Government of White domination. People
who live in poverty cannot be expected to pay rents under threats
of criminal prosecution and imprisonment. Above all, those who
are oppressed cannot tolerate a situation where their own people
man and maintain the machinery of their own national oppression.
Africans cannot serve on school boards and school committees
which are part of the Nationalists' Bantu Education. This is meant
to deprive Africans of true education.

Only traitors can serve on tribal councils. These are a mockery
of self-government. They are meant to keep us forever in a state of
slavery to Whites. We shall fight together tooth and nail, against
the Government plan to bring Bantu Authorities to the cities,
just as our people in the rural areas have fought.

Africans cannot continue to carry passes. Thousands of our
people are sent away to jail every month under the pass laws.

We shall ask our millions of friends outside South Africa to
intensify the boycott and isolation of the Government of this
country, diplomatically, economically, and in every other way.
The mines, industries, and farms of this country cannot carry on
without the labour of Africans imported from elsewhere in Africa.

We are the people of this country. We produce the wealth of the
gold mines, of the farms, and of industry. Non-collaboration is
the weapon we must use to bring down the Government. We have
decided to use it fully and without reservation.

June 1961

12

Editor's note

THE strike and post-strike events sharpened the teeth of African resistance but sharpened, too, the demand among sections of the Whites for reform. The cry for a National Convention was taken up by important leaders of opinion. For a while the Convention campaign shook the Government and its apartheid policies.

Mandela was still living and working underground.

On South African Freedom Day, 26 June, he released a post-strike letter.

LETTER FROM UNDERGROUND

THE magnificent response to the call of the National Action Council for a three-day strike and the wonderful work done by our organizers and field workers throughout the country proves once again that no power on earth can stop an oppressed people determined to win freedom.

Today is 26 June, a day known throughout the length and breadth of our country as Freedom Day. It is fit and proper that on this historic day I should speak to you and announce fresh plans for the opening of the second phase in the fight against the Verwoerd Republic, and for a National Convention.

You will remember that the Pietermaritzburg resolutions warned that if the Government did not call a National Convention before the end of May 1961, Africans, Coloureds, Indians, and European democrats would be asked not to collaborate with the Republic or any Government based on force. On several occasions since then the National Action Council explained that the last strike marked the beginning of a relentless mass struggle for the defeat of the Nationalist Government, and for a sovereign multi-racial convention. We stressed that the strike would be followed by other forms of mass pressure to force the race maniacs who govern our beloved country to make way for a democratic government of the people, by the people, and for the people. A full-scale and country-wide campaign of non-cooperation with the Government will be launched immediately. The precise form of the contemplated actions, its scope and dimensions and duration, will be announced to you at the appropriate time.

At the present moment it is sufficient to say that we plan to make government impossible. Those who are voteless cannot be expected to continue paying taxes to a Government which is not responsible to them. People who live in poverty and starvation cannot be expected to pay exorbitant house rents to the Government and local authorities. We furnish the sinews of agriculture and industry. We produce the work of the gold mines, the diamonds and the coal, of the farms and industry, in return for miserable wages. Why should we continue enriching those who steal the products of our sweat and blood? Those who exploit us and refuse us the rights to organize trade unions? Those who side with the Government when we stage peaceful demonstrations to assert our claims and aspirations? How can Africans serve on school boards and committees which are part of Bantu Education, a sinister scheme of the Nationalist Government to deprive the African people of real education in return for tribal education? Can Africans be expected to be content with serving on advisory boards and Bantu Authorities when the demand all over the continent of Africa is for national independence and self-government? Is it not an affront to the African people that the Government should now seek to extend Bantu Authorities to the cities, when people in the rural areas have refused to accept the same system and fought against it tooth and nail? Which African does not burn with indignation when thousands of our people are sent to jail every month under the cruel pass laws? Why should we continue carrying these badges of slavery? Non-collaboration is a dynamic weapon. We must refuse. We must use it to send this Government to the grave. It must be used vigorously and without delay. The entire resources of the Black people must be mobilized to withdraw all cooperation with the Nationalist Government.

Various forms of industrial and economic action will be employed to undermine the already tottering economy of the country. We will call upon the international bodies to expel South Africa and upon nations of the world to sever economic and diplomatic relations with the country.

I am informed that a warrant for my arrest has been issued, and that the police are looking for me. The National Action Council has given full and serious consideration to this question, and has sought the advice of many trusted friends and bodies and they have advised me not to surrender myself. I have accepted this advice, and will not give myself up to a Government I do not recognize. Any serious politician will realize that under present-day conditions in this country, to seek for cheap martyrdom by handing myself to the police is naïve and criminal. We have an important programme before us and it is important to carry it out very seriously and without delay.

I have chosen this latter course which is more difficult and which entails more risk and hardship than sitting in jail. I have had to separate myself from my dear wife and children, from my mother and sisters, to live as an outlaw in my own land. I have had to close my business, to abandon my profession, and live in poverty and misery, as many of my people are doing. I will continue to act as the spokesman of the National Action Council during the phase that is unfolding and in the tough struggles that lie ahead. I shall fight the Government side by side with you, inch by inch, and mile by mile, until victory is won. What are you going to do? Will you come along with us, or are you going to co-operate with the Government in its efforts to suppress the claims and aspirations of your own people? Or are you going to remain silent and neutral in a matter of life and death to my people, to our people? For my own part I have made my choice. I will not leave South Africa, nor will I surrender. Only through hardship, sacrifice, and militant action can freedom be won. The struggle is my life. I will continue fighting for freedom until the end of my days.

26 June 1961

13

MANDELA'S decision to remain underground to prepare new fighting forces was indicative of a new mood sweeping the African people. The Government mobilization to smash the strike had been a turning point in the country. Africans decided that the violence of the State made peaceful protest futile. In December 1961 the first acts of sabotage announced the formation of Umkonto we Sizwe (The Spear of the Nation).

Early in 1962 Mandela made a surprise appearance as the leader of the African National Congress delegation to the Addis Ababa conference of the Pan-African Freedom Movement of East and Central Africa. He had left South Africa—temporarily—to convey personally to Africa news of the crisis developing at home, and the decision to embark upon violent forms of struggle.

A LAND RULED BY THE GUN

THE delegation of the African National Congress, and I particularly, feel specially honoured by the invitation addressed to our organization by the PAFMECA to attend this historic conference and to participate in its deliberations and decisions. The extension of the PAFMECA area to South Africa, the heart and core of imperialist reaction, should mark the beginning of a new phase in the drive for the total liberation of Africa—a phase which derives special significance from the entry into PAFMECA of the independent States of Ethiopia, Somalia, and Sudan.

It was not without reason, we believe, that the Secretariat of PAFMECA chose as the seat of this conference the great country of Ethiopia, which, with hundreds of years of colourful history

behind it, can rightly claim to have paid the full price of freedom
and independence. His Imperial Majesty, himself a rich and
unfailing fountain of wisdom, has been foremost in promoting the
cause of unity, independence, and progress in Africa, as was so
amply demonstrated in the address he graciously delivered in
opening this assembly. The deliberations of our conference will
thus proceed in a setting most conducive to a scrupulous examination of the issues that are before us.

At the outset, our delegation wishes to place on record our
sincere appreciation of the relentless efforts made by the Independent African States and national movements in Africa and other
parts of the world, to help the African people in South Africa in
their just struggle for freedom and independence.

The movement for the boycott of South African goods and for
the imposition of economic and diplomatic sanctions against
South Africa has served to highlight most effectively the despotic
structure of the power that rules South Africa, and has given
tremendous inspiration to the liberation movement in our country.
It is particularly gratifying to note that the four independent
African States which are part of this conference, namely, Ethiopia,
Somalia, Sudan, and Tanganyika, are enforcing diplomatic and
economic sanctions against South Africa. We also thank all those
States that have given asylum and assistance to South African
refugees of all shades of political beliefs and opinion. The warm
affection with which South African freedom fighters are received
by democratic countries all over the world, and the hospitality so
frequently showered upon us by governments and political
organizations, has made it possible for some of our people to
escape persecution by the South African Government, to travel
freely from country to country, and from continent to continent, to
canvass our point of view and to rally support for our cause. We
are indeed extremely grateful for this spontaneous demonstration
of solidarity and support, and sincerely hope that each and every
one of us will prove worthy of the trust and confidence the world
has in us.

We believe that one of the main objectives of this conference is
to work out concrete plans to speed up the struggle for the
liberation of those territories in this region that are still under
alien rule. In most of these territories the imperialist forces have

been considerably weakened and are unable to resist the demand for freedom and independence—thanks to the powerful blows delivered by the freedom movements.

Although the national movements must remain alert and vigilant against all forms of imperialist intrigue and deception, there can be no doubt that imperialism is in full retreat and the attainment of independence by many of these countries has become an almost accomplished fact. Elsewhere, notably in South Africa, the liberation movement faces formidable difficulties and the struggle is likely to be long, complicated, hard, and bitter, requiring maximum unity of the national movement inside the country, and calling for level and earnest thinking on the part of its leaders, for skilful planning and intensive organization.

South Africa is known throughout the world as a country where the most fierce forms of colour discrimination are practised, and where the peaceful struggles of the African people for freedom are violently suppressed. It is a country torn from top to bottom by fierce racial strife and conflict and where the blood of African patriots frequently flows.

Almost every African household in South Africa knows about the massacre of our people at Bulhoek in the Queenstown district where detachments of the army and police, armed with artillery, machine-guns, and rifles, opened fire on unarmed Africans, killing 163 persons, wounding 129, and during which 95 people were arrested simply because they refused to move from a piece of land on which they lived.

Almost every African family remembers a similar massacre of our African brothers in South-West Africa when the South African Government assembled aeroplanes, heavy machine-guns, artillery, and rifles, killing 100 people and mutilating scores of others, merely because the Bondelswart people refused to pay dog tax.

On 1 May 1950, 18 Africans were shot dead by the police in Johannesburg whilst striking peacefully for higher wages. The massacre at Sharpeville in March 1960 is a matter of common knowledge and is still fresh in our minds. According to a statement in Parliament made by C. R. Swart, then Minister for Justice, between May 1948 and March 1954, 104 Africans were killed and 248 wounded by the police in the course of political demonstrations. By the middle of June 1960, these figures had risen to well over 300 killed and 500 wounded. Naked force and violence is the weapon openly used by the South African Government to beat down the struggles of the African people and to suppress their aspirations.

The repressive policies of the South African Government are reflected not only in the number of those African martyrs who perished from guns and bullets, but in the merciless persecution of all political leaders and in the total repression of political opposition. Persecution of political leaders and suppression of political organizations became ever more violent under the Nationalist Party Government. From 1952 the Government used its legal powers to launch a full-scale attack on leaders of the African National Congress. Many of its prominent members were ordered by the Government to resign permanently from it and never again participate in its activities. Others were prohibited from attending gatherings for specified periods ranging up to five years. Many were confined to certain districts, banished from their homes and families and even deported from the country.

In December 1956, Chief A. J. Lutuli, president-general of the ANC, was arrested together with 155 other freedom fighters and charged with treason. The trial which then followed is unprecedented in the history of the country, both in its magnitude and duration. It dragged on for over four years and drained our resources to the limit. In March 1960 after the murderous killing of about seventy Africans in Sharpeville, a state of emergency was declared and close on 20,000 people were detained without trial. Even as we meet here today, martial law prevails throughout the territory of the Transkei, an area of 16,000 square miles with an African population of nearly 2,500,000. The Government stubbornly refuses to publish the names and number of persons detained. But it is estimated that close on 2,000 Africans are presently languishing in jail in this area alone. Amongst these are to be found teachers, lawyers, doctors, clerks, workers from the towns, peasants from the country, and other freedom fighters. In this same area and during the last six months, more than thirty Africans have been sentenced to death by White judicial officers, hostile to our aspirations, for offences arising out of political demonstrations.

On 26 August 1961 the South African Government even openly defied the British Government when its police crossed into the neighbouring British protectorate of Basutoland and kidnapped Anderson Ganyile, one of the country's rising freedom stars, who led the Pondo people's memorable struggles against apartheid tribal rule.

Apart from these specific instances, there are numerous other South African patriots, known and unknown, who have been sacrificed in various ways on the altar of African freedom.

This is but a brief and sketchy outline of the momentous struggle of the freedom fighters in our country, of the sacrifice they have made and of the price that is being paid at the present moment by those who keep the freedom flag flying.

For years our political organizations have been subjected to vicious attack by the Government. In 1957 there was considerable mass unrest and disturbances in the country districts of Zeerest, Sekhukhuniland, and Rustenburg. In all these areas there was widespread dissatisfaction with Government policy and there were revolts against the pass laws, the poll tax, and Government-inspired tribal authorities. Instead of meeting the legitimate political demands of the masses of the people and redressing their grievances, the Government reacted by banning the ANC in all these districts. In April 1960 the Government went further and completely outlawed both the African National Congress and the Pan-Africanist Congress. By resorting to these drastic methods the Government had hoped to silence all opposition to its harsh policies and to remove all threats to the privileged position of the Whites in the country. It had hoped for days of perfect peace and comfort for White South Africa, free from revolt and revolution. It believed that through its strong-arm measures it could achieve what White South Africa has failed to accomplish during the last fifty years, namely, to compel Africans to accept the position that in our country freedom and happiness are the preserve of the White man.

But uneasy lies the head that wears the crown of White supremacy in South Africa. The banning and confinement of leaders, banishments and deportations, imprisonment and even death, has never deterred South African patriots. The very same day it was outlawed, the ANC issued a public statement announcing that it would definitely defy the Government's ban and carry out operations from underground. The people of South Africa have adopted this declaration as their own and South Africa is today a land of turmoil and conflict.

In May last year a general strike was called. In the history of our country no strike has ever been organized under such formidable difficulties and dangers. The odds against us were tremendous. Our organizations were outlawed. Special legislation had been rushed through Parliament empowering the Government to round up its political opponents and to detain them without trial. One week before the strike, 10,000 Africans were arrested and kept in jail until after the strike. All meetings were banned throughout the country and our field workers were trailed and hounded by members of the Security Branch. General mobilization was ordered throughout the country and every available White man and woman was put under arms. An English periodical described the situation on the eve of the strike in the following terms:

'In the country's biggest call-up since the war, scores of citizens' force and commando units were mobilized in the big towns. Camps were established at strategic points; heavy army vehicles carrying equipment and supplies moved in a steady stream along the Reef; helicopters hovered over African residential areas and trained searchlights on houses, yards, lands, and unlit areas. Hundreds of White civilians were sworn in as special constables, hundreds of white women spent weekends in shooting at targets. Gun shops sold out of their stocks of revolvers and ammunition. All police leave was cancelled throughout the country. Armed guards were posted to protect power stations and other sources of essential services. Saracen armoured cars and troop carriers patrolled townships. Police vans patrolled areas and broadcast statements that Africans who struck work would be sacked and endorsed out of the town.'

This was the picture in South Africa on the eve of the general strike, but our people stood up to the test most magnificently. The response was less than we expected but we made solid and substantial achievements. Hundreds of thousands of workers stayed away from work and the country's industries and commerce were seriously damaged. Hundreds of thousands of students and schoolchildren did not go to school for the duration of the strike.

The celebrations which had been planned by the Government to mark the inauguration of the Republic were not only completely boycotted by the Africans, but were held in an atmosphere of tension and crisis in which the whole country looked like a military camp in a state of unrest and uncertainty. This panic-stricken show of force was a measure of the power of the liberation movement and yet it failed to stem the rising tide of popular discontent.

How strong is the freedom struggle in South Africa today? What role should PAFMECA play to strengthen the liberation movement in South Africa and speed up the liberation of our country? These are questions frequently put by those who have our welfare at heart.

The view has been expressed in some quarters outside South Africa that, in the special situation obtaining in our country, our people will never win freedom through their own efforts. Those who hold this view point to the formidable apparatus of force and coercion in the hands of the Government, to the size of its armies, the fierce suppression of civil liberties, and the persecution of political opponents of the régime. Consequently, in these quarters, we are urged to look for our salvation beyond our borders.

Nothing could be further from the truth.

It is true that world opinion against the policies of the South African Government has hardened considerably in recent years. The All African People's Conference held in Accra in 1958, the Positive Action Conference for Peace and Security in Africa, also held in Accra in April 1960, the Conference of Independent African States held in this famous capital in June of the same year, and the conferences at Casablanca and Monrovia last year, as well as the Lagos Conference this month, passed militant resolutions in which they sharply condemned and rejected the racial policies of the South African Government. It has become clear to us that the whole of Africa is unanimously behind the move to ensure effective economic and diplomatic sanctions against the South African Government.

At the international level, concrete action against South Africa found expression in the expulsion of South Africa from the Commonwealth, which was achieved with the active initiative and collaboration of the African members of the Commonwealth. These were Ghana, Nigeria, and Tanganyika (although the latter had not yet achieved its independence). Nigeria also took the initiative in moving for the expulsion of South Africa from the International Labour Organization. But most significant was the draft resolution tabled at the fifteenth session of the United Nations which called for sanctions against South Africa. This resolution had the support of all the African members of the United Nations, with only one exception. The significance of the draft was not minimized by the fact that a milder resolution was finally adopted calling for individual or collective sanctions by member states. At the sixteenth session of the United Nations last year, the African states played a marvellous role in successfully carrying through the General Assembly a resolution against the address delivered by the South African Minister of Foreign Affairs, Mr Eric Louw, and subsequently in the moves calling for the expulsion of South Africa from the United Nations and for sanctions against her. Although the United Nations itself has neither expelled nor adopted sanctions against South Africa, many independent African States are in varying degrees enforcing economic and other sanctions against her. This increasing world pressure on South Africa has greatly weakened her international position and given a tremendous impetus to the freedom struggle inside the country. No less a danger to White minority rule and a guarantee of ultimate victory for us is the freedom struggle that is raging furiously beyond the borders of the South African territory; the rapid progress of Kenya, Uganda, and Zanzibar towards independence; the victories gained by the Nyasaland Malawi Congress; the unabated determination of Kenneth Kaunda's UNIP; the courage displayed by the freedom fighters of the ZAPU, successor to the now banned NDP; the gallantry of the African crusaders in the Angolan war of liberation and the storm clouds forming around the excesses of Portuguese repression in Moçambique; the growing power of the independence movements in South-West Africa and the emergence of powerful political organizations in the High Commission territories—all these are forces which cannot compromise with White domination anywhere.

But we believe it would be fatal to create the illusion that external pressures render it unnecessary for us to tackle the enemy from within. The centre and cornerstone of the struggle for freedom and democracy in South Africa lies inside South Africa itself. Apart from those required for essential work outside the country, freedom fighters are in great demand for work inside the country. We owe it as a duty to ourselves and to the freedom-loving peoples of the world to build and maintain in South Africa itself a powerful, solid movement, capable of surviving any attack by the Government and sufficiently militant to fight back with a determination that comes from the knowledge and conviction that it is first and foremost by our own struggle and sacrifice inside South Africa itself that victory over White domination and apartheid can be won.

The struggle in the areas still subject to imperialist rule can be delayed and even defeated if it is uncoordinated. Only by our combined efforts and united action can we repulse the multiple onslaughts of the imperialists and fight our way to victory. Our enemies fight collectively and combine to exploit our people.

The clear examples of collective imperialism have made themselves felt more and more in our region by the formation of an unholy alliance between the Governments of South Africa, Portugal, and the so-called Central African Federation. Hence these governments openly and shamelessly gave military assistance consisting of personnel and equipment to the traitorous Tshombe régime in Katanga.

At this very moment it has been widely reported that a secret defence agreement has been signed between Portugal, South Africa, and the Federation, following visits of Federation and South African defence ministers to Lisbon; the Federation defence minister to Luanda, and South African Defence Ministry delegations to Moçambique. Dr Salazar was quoted in the Johannesburg *Star* of 8 July 1961 as saying: 'Our relations—Moçambique's and Angola's on the one hand and the Federation and South Africa on the other—arise from the existence of our common borders and our traditional friendships that unite our Governments and our people. Our mutual interests are manifold and we are conscious of the need to cooperate to fulfil our common needs.'

Last year, Southern Rhodesian troops were training in South Africa and so were RAF units. A military mission from South Africa and another from the Rhodesia Federation visited Lourenço Marques in Moçambique, at the invitation of the Moçambique Army Command, and took part in training exercises in which several units totalling 2,600 men participated. These operations included dropping exercises for paratroopers.

A report in a South African aviation magazine, *Wings* (December 1961), states: 'The Portuguese are hastily building nine new aerodromes in Portuguese East Africa (Moçambique) following their troubles in Angola. The new 'dromes are all capable of taking jet fighters and are situated along or near the borders of Tanganyika and Nyasaland,' and gives full details.

Can anyone, therefore, doubt the role that the freedom movements should play in view of this hideous conspiracy?

As we have stated earlier, the freedom movement in South Africa believes that hard and swift blows should be delivered with the full weight of the masses of the people, who alone furnish us with one absolute guarantee that the freedom flames now burning in the country shall never be extinguished.

During the last ten years the African people in South Africa have fought many freedom battles, involving civil disobedience, strikes, protest marches, boycotts and demonstrations of all kinds. In all these campaigns we repeatedly stressed the importance of discipline, peaceful and non-violent struggle. We did so, firstly because we felt that there were still opportunities for peaceful struggle and we sincerely worked for peaceful changes. Secondly, we did not want to expose our people to situations where they might become easy targets for the trigger-happy police of South Africa. But the situation has now radically altered.

South Africa is now a land ruled by the gun. The Government is increasing the size of its army, of the navy, of its air force, and the police. Pill-boxes and road blocks are being built up all over the country. Armament factories are being set up in Johannesburg and other cities. Officers of the South African army have visited Algeria and Angola where they were briefed exclusively on methods of suppressing popular struggles. All opportunities for peaceful agitation and struggle have been closed. Africans no longer have the freedom even to stay peacefully in their houses in protest against the oppressive policies of the Government. During the strike in May last year the police went from house to house, beating up Africans and driving them to work.

Hence it is understandable why today many of our people are turning their faces away from the path of peace and non-violence. They feel that peace in our country must be considered already broken when a minority Government maintains its authority over the majority by force and violence.

A crisis is developing in earnest in South Africa. However, no high command ever announces beforehand what its strategy and tactics will be to meet a situation. Certainly, the days of civil disobedience, of strikes, and mass demonstrations are not over and we will resort to them over and over again.

But a leadership commits a crime against its own people if it hesitates to sharpen its political weapons which have become less effective.

Regarding the actual situation pertaining today in South Africa I should mention that I have just come out of South Africa, having for the last ten months lived in my own country as an outlaw, away from family and friends. When I was compelled to lead this sort of life, I made a public statement in which I announced that I would not leave the country but would continue working underground. I meant it and I have honoured that undertaking. But when my organization received the invitation to this conference it was decided that I should attempt to come out and attend the conference to furnish the various African leaders, leading sons of our continent, with the most up-to-date information about the situation.

During the past ten months I moved up and down my country and spoke to peasants in the countryside, to workers in the cities, to students and professional people. It dawned on me quite clearly that the situation had become explosive. It was not surprising therefore when one morning in October last year we woke up to read Press reports of widespread sabotage involving the cutting of telephone wires and the blowing up of power pylons. The Government remained unshaken and White South Africa tried to dismiss it as the work of criminals. Then on the night of 16 December last year the whole of South Africa vibrated under the heavy blows of UMKONTO WE SIZWE (The Spear of the Nation). Government buildings were blasted with explosives in Johannesburg, the industrial heart of South Africa, in Port Elizabeth, and in Durban. It was now clear that this was a political demonstration of a formidable kind, and the Press announced the beginning of planned acts of sabotage in the country. It was still a small beginning because a Government as strong and as aggressive as that of South Africa can never be induced to part with political power by bomb explosions in one night and in three cities only. But in a country where freedom fighters frequently pay with their very lives and at a time when the most elaborate military preparations are being made to crush the people's struggles, planned acts of sabotage against Government installations introduce a new phase in the political situation and are a demonstration of the people's unshakeable determination to win freedom whatever the cost may be. The Government is preparing to strike viciously at political leaders and freedom fighters. But the people will not take these blows sitting down.

In such a grave situation it is fit and proper that this conference of PAFMECA should sound a clarion call to the struggling peoples in South Africa and other dependent areas, to close ranks, to stand firm as a rock and not allow themselves to be divided by petty political rivalries whilst their countries burn. At this critical moment in the history of struggle, unity amongst our people in South Africa and in the other territories has become as vital as the air we breathe and it should be preserved at all costs.

Finally, dear friends, I should assure you that the African people of South Africa, notwithstanding fierce persecution and untold suffering, in their ever-increasing courage will not for one single moment be diverted from the historic mission of liberating their country and winning freedom lasting peace, and happiness.

We are confident that in the decisive struggles ahead, our liberation movement will receive the fullest support of PAFMECA and of all freedom-loving people throughout the world.

Addis Ababa
January 1962

ON TRIAL

14

Editor's note

FROM Addis Ababa and highly successful talks with African Heads of State and Opposition leaders in Britain, Mandela returned to live 'somewhere in South Africa'.

He came to be known as the 'Black Pimpernel' and fact and fancy were joined in the stories about his daring that circulated in African townships. But seventeen months after he had gone underground he was caught by the police, as a result of the work of a police informer.

In the trial that followed, Mandela was charged on two counts: inciting African workers to strike (the March 1961 stay-at-home); and leaving South Africa without a valid travel document. He turned the trial into a scathing indictment of White domination.

The following is an almost complete account of the trial held in Pretoria at the Old Synagogue (converted into a courtroom) where less than two years earlier Mandela and twenty-eight others had been acquitted in the Treason Trial. The trial opened on 22 October 1962 after several false starts occasioned by police efforts to hamper Mandela's chances of obtaining legal defence and manoeuvres to hold the trial not in Johannesburg, Mandela's home city and seat of his strongest urban support, but in Pretoria, the Nationalist Party capital.

BLACK MAN IN A WHITE COURT

YOUR WORSHIP, I have elected to conduct my own defence. Some time during the progress of these proceedings, I hope to be able to indicate that this case is a trial of the aspirations of the African people, and because of that I thought it proper to conduct my own defence.

I have an application to address to Your Worship. At the outset, I want to make it perfectly clear that the remarks I am going to make are not addressed to Your Worship in his personal capacity, nor are they intended to reflect upon the integrity of the Court.

The point I wish to raise in my argument is based not on personal considerations, but on important questions that go beyond the scope of this present trial. I might also mention that in the course of this application I am frequently going to refer to the White man and the White people. I want at once to make it clear that I am no racialist, and I detest racialism, because I regard it as a barbaric thing, whether it comes from a Black man or from a White man. The terminology that I am going to employ will be compelled on me by the nature of the application I am making.

I want to apply for Your Worship's recusal from this case. I challenge the right of this Court to hear my case on two grounds.

Firstly, I challenge it because I fear that I will not be given a fair and proper trial. Secondly, I consider myself neither legally nor morally bound to obey laws made by a Parliament in which I have no representation.

In a political trial such as this one, which involves a clash of the aspirations of the African people and those of Whites, the country's courts, as presently constituted, cannot be impartial and fair.

In such cases, Whites are interested parties. To have a White judicial officer presiding, however high his esteem, and however strong his sense of fairness and justice, is to make Whites judges in their own case.

It is improper and against the elementary principles of justice to entrust Whites with cases involving the denial by them of basic human rights to the African people.

What sort of justice is this that enables the aggrieved to sit in judgement over those against whom they have laid a charge?

A judiciary controlled entirely by Whites and enforcing laws enacted by a White Parliament in which Africans have no representation—laws which in most cases are passed in the face of unanimous opposition from Africans—

Here the Magistrate interrupted

The Universal Declaration of Human Rights provides that all men are equal before the law and are entitled, without any discrimination, to equal protection of the law.

In May 1951, Dr D. F. Malan, then Prime Minister, told the Union Parliament that this provision of the Declaration applied in this country. Similar statements have been made on numerous occasions in the past by prominent Whites in this country, including judges and magistrates.

But the real truth is that there is in fact no equality before the law whatsoever as far as our people are concerned, and statements to the contrary are definitely incorrect and misleading.

It is true that an African who is charged in a court of law enjoys, on the surface, the same rights and privileges as an accused who is White in so far as the conduct of this trial is concerned. He is governed by the same rules of procedure and evidence as apply to a White accused. But it would be grossly inaccurate to conclude from this fact that an African consequently enjoys equality before the law.

In its proper meaning equality before the law means the right to participate in the making of the laws by which one is governed, a constitution which guarantees democratic rights to all sections of the population, the right to approach the court for protection or relief in the case of the violation of rights guaranteed in the constitution, and the right to take part in the administration of justice as judges, magistrates, attorneys-general, law advisers, and similar positions.

In the absence of these safeguards the phrase 'equality before the law', in so far as it is intended to apply to us, is meaningless and misleading. All the rights and privileges to which I have referred are monopolized by Whites, and we enjoy none of them.

The White man makes all the laws, he drags us before his courts and accuses us, and he sits in judgement over us.

It is fit and proper to raise the question sharply, what is this rigid colour-bar in the administration of justice? Why is it that in this courtroom I face a White magistrate, confronted by a White prosecutor, and escorted into the dock by a White orderly? Can anyone honestly and seriously suggest that in this type of atmosphere the scales of justice are evenly balanced?

Why is it that no African in the history of this country has ever had the honour of being tried by his own kith and kin, by his own flesh and blood?

I will tell Your Worship why: the real purpose of this rigid

colour-bar is to ensure that the justice dispensed by the courts
should conform to the policy of the country, however much that
policy might be in conflict with the norms of justice accepted in
judiciaries throughout the civilized world.

I feel oppressed by the atmosphere of White domination that
lurks all around in this courtroom. Somehow this atmosphere calls
to mind the inhuman injustices caused to my people outside this
courtroom by this same White domination.

It reminds me that I am voteless because there is a Parliament in
this country that is White-controlled. I am without land because
the White minority has taken a lion's share of my country and
forced me to occupy poverty-stricken Reserves, over-populated
and over-stocked. We are ravaged by starvation and disease. . . .

Interruption by the Magistrate

How can I be expected to believe that this same race discrimination, which has been the cause of so much injustice and suffering
right through the years, should now operate here to give me a fair
and proper trial? Is there no danger that an African may regard
these courts, not as impartial tribunals dispensing justice without
fear or favour, but as instruments used by the White man to
punish those among us who clamour for deliverance from the
fiery furnace of White rule?

I have grave fears that this system of justice may enable the
guilty to drag the innocent before the courts. It enables the
unjust to prosecute and demand vengeance against the just.

This is the first ground of my objection: that I will not be given
a fair and proper trial.

The second ground of my objection is that I consider myself
neither morally nor legally obliged to obey laws made by a
Parliament in which I am not represented.

That the will of the people is the basis of the authority of
government is a principle universally acknowledged as sacred
throughout the civilized world, and constitutes the basic foundations of freedom and justice. It is understandable why citizens,
who have the vote as well as the right of direct representation in
the country's governing bodies, should be morally and legally
bound by the laws governing the country.

It would be equally understandable why we, as Africans, should adopt the attitude that we are neither morally nor legally bound to obey laws which we have not made, nor can we be expected to have confidence in courts which enforce such laws.

I am aware that in many cases of this nature in the past, South African courts have upheld the right of the African people to work for democratic changes. Some of our judicial officers have even openly criticized the policy which refuses to acknowledge that all men are born free and equal, and fearlessly condemned the denial of opportunities to our people.

But such exceptions exist in spite of, not because of, the grotesque system of justice that has been built up in this country. These exceptions furnish yet another proof that even among the country's Whites there are honest men whose sense of fairness and justice revolts against the cruelty perpetrated by their own White brothers to our people.

The existence of genuine democratic values among some of the country's Whites in the judiciary, however slender they may be, is welcomed by me. But I have no illusions about the significance of this fact, healthy a sign as it might be. Such honest and upright Whites are few and they have certainly not succeeded in convincing the vast majority of the rest of the White population that White supremacy leads to dangers and disaster.

However, it would be a hopeless commandant who relied for his victories on the few soldiers in the enemy camp who sympathize with his cause. A competent general pins his faith on the superior striking power he commands and on the justness of his cause which he must pursue uncompromisingly to the bitter end.

I hate race discrimination most intensely and in all its manifestations. I have fought it all during my life; I fight it now, and will do so until the end of my days. Even although I now happen to be tried by one whose opinion I hold in high esteem, I detest most violently the set-up that surrounds me here. It makes me feel that I am a Black man in a White man's court. This should not be. I should feel perfectly at ease and at home with the assurance that I am being tried by a fellow South African who does not regard me as an inferior, entitled to a special type of justice.

This is not the type of atmosphere most conducive to feelings of security and confidence in the impartiality of a court.

The Court might reply to this part of my argument by assuring me that it will try my case fairly and without fear or favour, that in deciding whether or not I am guilty of the offence charged by the State, the Court will not be influenced by the colour of my skin or by any other improper motive.

That might well be so. But such a reply would completely miss the point of my argument.

As already indicated, my objection is not directed to Your Worship in his personal capacity, nor is it intended to reflect upon the integrity of the Court. My objection is based upon the fact that our courts, as presently constituted, create grave doubts in the minds of an African accused, whether he will receive a fair and proper trial.

This doubt springs from objective facts relating to the practice of unfair discrimination against the Black man in the constitution of the country's courts. Such doubts cannot be allayed by mere verbal assurances from a presiding officer, however sincere such assurances might be. There is only one way, and one way only, of allaying such doubts, namely, by removing unfair discrimination in judicial appointments. This is my first difficulty.

I have yet another difficulty about similar assurances Your Worship might give. Broadly speaking, Africans and Whites in this country have no common standard of fairness, morality, and ethics, and it would be very difficult to determine on my part what standard of fairness and justice Your Worship has in mind.

In their relationship with us, South African Whites regard it as fair and just to pursue policies which have outraged the conscience of mankind and of honest and upright men throughout the civilized world. They suppress our aspirations, bar our way to freedom, and deny us opportunities to promote our moral and material progress, to secure ourselves from fear and want. All the good things of life are reserved for the White folk and we Blacks are expected to be content to nourish our bodies with such pieces of food as drop from the tables of men with White skins. This is the White man's standard of justice and fairness. Herein lies his conception of ethics. Whatever he himself may say in his defence, the White man's moral standards in this country must be judged by the extent to which he has condemned the vast majority of its inhabitants to serfdom and inferiority.

We, on the other hand, regard the struggle against colour

discrimination and for the pursuit of freedom and happiness as the highest aspiration of all men. Through bitter experience, we have learnt to regard the White man as a harsh and merciless type of human being whose contempt for our rights, and whose utter indifference to the promotion of our welfare, makes his assurances to us absolutely meaningless and hypocritical.

I have the hope and confidence that Your Worship will not hear this objection lightly nor regard it as frivolous. I have decided to speak frankly and honestly because the injustice I have referred to contains the seeds of an extremely dangerous situation for our country and people. I make no threat when I say that unless these wrongs are remedied without delay, we might well find that even plain talk before the country's courts is too timid a method to draw the attention of the country to our political demands.

The application for the recusal of the Magistrate was refused.

Among the persons to take the stand in the witness-box was Mr Barnard, private secretary to the Prime Minister, Dr H. F. Verwoerd.

Mr Barnard handed into court two letters written by Mandela to the Prime Minister demanding a National Convention before 31 May 1961, the date of the founding of the Republic of South Africa. The witness alleged that Dr Verwoerd had passed the letters on to the Minister of Justice. He did not think it improper of Dr Verwoerd not to send a reply on the issues raised in the letters.

In his cross-examination of this witness, Mandela first read the contents of Exhibit 17, being a letter he had addressed to the Prime Minister:

I am directed by the All-In African National Action Council to address your Government in the following terms:

The All-In African National Action Council was established in terms of a resolution adopted at a conference held at Pietermaritzburg on 25 and 26 March 1961. This conference was attended by 1,500 delegates from town and country, representing 145 religious, social, cultural, sporting, and political bodies.

Conference noted that your Government, after receiving a mandate from a section of the European population, decided to proclaim a Republic on 31 May.

It was the firm view of delegates that your Government, which represents only a minority of the population in this country, is not entitled to take such a decision without first seeking the views and obtaining the express consent of the African people. Conference feared that under this proposed Republic your Government, which is already notorious the world over for its obnoxious policies, would continue to make even more savage attacks on the rights and living conditions of the African people.

Conference carefully considered the grave political situation facing the African people today. Delegate after delegate drew attention to the vicious manner in which your Government forced the people of Zeerust, Sekhukhuniland, Pondoland, Nongoma, Tembuland and other areas to accept the unpopular system of Bantu Authorities, and pointed to numerous facts and incidents which indicate the rapid manner in which race relations are deteriorating in this country.

It was the earnest opinion of Conference that this dangerous situation could be averted only by the calling of a sovereign national convention representative of all South Africans, to draw up a new non-racial and democratic Constitution. Such a convention would discuss our national problems in a sane and sober manner, and would work out solutions which sought to preserve and safeguard the interests of all sections of the population.

Conference unanimously decided to call upon your Government to summon such a convention before 31 May.

Conference further decided that unless your Government calls the convention before the above-mentioned date, country-wide demonstrations would be held on the eve of the Republic in protest. Conference also resolved that in addition to the demonstrations, the African people would be called upon to refuse to co-operate with the proposed Republic.

We attach the Resolutions of the Conference for your attention and necessary action.

We now demand that your Government call the convention before 31 May, failing which we propose to adopt the steps indicated in paragraphs 8 and 9 of this letter.

These demonstrations will be conducted in a disciplined and peaceful manner.

We are fully aware of the implications of this decision, and the action we propose taking. We have no illusions about the counter-measures your Government might take in this matter. After all, South Africa and the world know that during the last thirteen years your Government has subjected us to merciless and arbitrary rule. Hundreds of our people have been banned and confined to certain areas. Scores have been banished to remote parts of the country, and many arrested and jailed for a multitude of offences. It has become extremely difficult to hold meetings, and freedom of speech has been drastically curtailed. During the last twelve months we have gone through a period of grim dictatorship, during which seventy-five people were killed and hundreds injured while peacefully demonstrating against passes.

Political organizations were declared unlawful, and thousands flung into jail without trial. Your Government can only take these measures to suppress the forthcoming demonstrations, and these measures have failed to stop opposition to the policies of your Government.

We are not deterred by threats of force and violence made by you and your Government, and will carry out our duty without flinching.

MANDELA: You remember the contents of this letter?

BARNARD: I do.

Q. Did you place this letter before your Prime Minister?

A. Yes.

Q. On what date? Can you remember?

A. It is difficult to remember, but I gather from the date specified on the date stamp, the Prime Minister's Office date stamp. . . .

Q. That is 24 April. Now was any reply given to this letter by the Prime Minister? Did he reply to this letter?

A. He did not reply to the writer.

Q. He did not reply to the letter. Now, will you agree that this letter raises matters of vital concern to the vast majority of the citizens of this country?

A. I do not agree.

Q. You don't agree? You don't agree that the question of human rights, of civil liberties, is a matter of vital importance to the African people?

A. Yes, that is so, indeed.

Q. Are these things mentioned here?

A. Yes, I think so.

Q. They are mentioned. You agree that this letter deals with matters of vital importance to the African people in this country? You have already agreed that this letter raises questions like the rights of freedom, civil liberties, and so on?

A. Yes, the letter raises it.

Q. Important questions to any citizen?

A. Yes.

Q. Now, you know of course that Africans don't enjoy the rights demanded in this letter. They are denied the rights of government?

A. Some rights.

Q. No African is a Member of Parliament?

A. That is right.

Q. No African can be a Member of the Provincial Council, of the Municipal Councils?

A. Yes.

Q. Africans have no vote in this country?

A. They have got no vote as far as Parliament is concerned.

Q. Yes, that is what I am talking about, I am talking about Parliament, and other government bodies of the country, the Provincial Councils, the Municipal Councils. They have no vote?

A. That is right.

Q. Would you agree with me that in any civilized country in the world it would be at least most scandalous for a Prime Minister to fail to reply to a letter raising vital issues affecting the majority of the citizens of that country. Would you agree with that?

A. I don't agree with that.

Q. You don't agree that it would be irregular for a Prime Minister to ignore a letter raising vital issues affecting the vast majority of the citizens of that country?

A. This letter has not been ignored by the Prime Minister.

Q. Just answer the question. Do you regard it proper for a Prime Minister not to respond to pleas made in regard to vital issues by the vast majority of the citizens of the country? You say that is not wrong?

A. The Prime Minister did respond to the letter.

Q. Mr Barnard, I don't want to be rude to you. Will you confine yourself to answering my questions? The question I am putting to you is, do you agree that it is most improper on the part of a Prime Minister not to reply to a communication raising vital issues affecting the vast majority of the country?

A.   I do not agree in this special case, because . . .

Q.   As a general proposition? Would you regard it as speaking—would you regard it as improper, speaking generally, for a Prime Minister not to respond to a letter of this nature, that is a letter raising vital issues affecting the majority of the citizens?

At this stage the prosecutor interrupted the proceedings by objecting to the line of questioning Mandela was pursuing.

MANDELA—*resuming:*

Q.   You say that the Prime Minister did not ignore this letter?

A.   He did not acknowledge the letter to the writer.

Q.   This letter was not ignored by the Prime Minister?

A.   No, it was not ignored.

Q.   It was attended to?

A.   It was indeed.

Q.   In what way?

A.   According to the usual procedure, and that is that the Prime Minister refers correspondence to the respective Minister, the Minister most responsible for that particular letter.

Q.   Was this letter referred to another Department?

A.   That is right.

Q.   Which Department?

A.   The Department of Justice.

Q.   Can you explain why I was not favoured with the courtesy of an acknowledgement of this letter, and also the explanation that it had been referred to the appropriate Department for attention?

A.   When a letter is replied to, and whether it should be replied to, depends on the contents of the letter in many instances.

Q.   My question is, can you explain to me why I was not favoured with the courtesy of an acknowledgement of the letter, irrespective of what the Prime Minister is going to do about it? Why was I not favoured with this courtesy?

A.   Because of the contents of this letter.

Q.   Because it raises vital issues?

A.   Because of the contents of the letter.

Q. I see. This is not the type of thing the Prime Minister would ever consider responding to?

A. The Prime Minister did respond.

Q. You say that the issues raised in this letter are not the type of thing your Prime Minister could ever respond to?

A. The whole tone of the letter was taken into consideration.

Q. The tone of the letter demanding a National Convention? Of all South Africans? That is the tone of the letter? That is not the type of thing your Prime Minister could ever respond to.

A. The tone of the letter indicates whether, and to what extent, the Prime Minister responds to correspondence.

MANDELA: I want to put it to you that in failing to respond to this letter, your Prime Minister fell below the standards which one expects from one in such a position.

Now this letter, Exhibit 18, is dated 26 June 1961, and it is also addressed to the Prime Minister, and it reads as follows:

I refer you to my letter of 20 April 1961, to which you do not have the courtesy to reply or acknowledge receipt. In the letter referred to above I informed you of the resolutions passed by the All-In African National Conference in Pietermaritzburg on 26 March 1961, demanding the calling by your Government before 31 May 1961 of a multi-racial and sovereign National Convention to draw up a new non-racial and democratic Constitution for South Africa. The Conference Resolution which was attached to my letter indicated that if your Government did not call this Convention by the specific date, country-wide demonstrations would be staged to mark our protest against the White Republic forcibly imposed on us by a minority. The Resolution further indicated that in addition to the demonstrations, the African people would be called upon not to cooperate with the Republican Government, or with any Government based on force. As your Government did not respond to our demands, All-In African National Council, which was entrusted by the Conference with the task of implementing its resolutions, called for a General Strike on the 29th, 30th, and 31st of last month. As predicted in my letter of 30 April 1961, your Government sought to suppress the strike by force. You rushed a special law in Parliament authorizing the detention without trial of people connected with the organization of the strike. The army was mobilized and European civilians armed. More than ten thousand innocent Africans were arrested under the pass laws and meetings banned throughout the country. Long before the factory gates were opened on Monday,

29 May 1961, senior police officers and Nationalist South Africans spread a deliberate falsehood and announced that the strike had failed. All these measures failed to break the strike and our people stood up magnificently and gave us solid and substantial support. Factory and office workers, businessmen in town and country, students in university colleges, in the primary and secondary schools, rose to the occasion and recorded in clear terms their opposition to the Republic. The Government is guilty of self-deception if they say that non-Europeans did not respond to the call. Considerations of honesty demand of your Government to realize that the African people who constitute four-fifths of the country's population are against your Republic. As indicated above, the Pietermaritzburg resolution provided that in addition to the country-wide demonstrations, the African people would refuse to cooperate with the Republic or any form of government based on force. Failure by your Government to call the Convention makes it imperative for us to launch a full-scale and country-wide campaign for non-cooperation with your Government. There are two alternatives before you. Either you accede to our demands and call a National Convention of all South Africans to draw up a democratic Constitution, which will end the frightful policies of racial oppression pursued by your Government. By pursuing this course and abandoning the repressive and dangerous policies of your Government, you may still save our country from economic dislocation and ruin and from civil strife and bitterness. Alternatively, you may choose to persist with the present policies which are cruel and dishonest and which are opposed by millions of people here and abroad. For our own part, we wish to make it perfectly clear that we shall never cease to fight against repression and injustice, and we are resuming active opposition against your régime. In taking this decision we must again stress that we have no illusions of the serious implications of our decision. We know that your Government will once again unleash all its fury and barbarity to persecute the African people. But as the result of the last strike has clearly proved, no power on earth can stop an oppressed people, determined to win their freedom. History punishes those who resort to force and fraud to suppress the claims and legitimate aspirations of the majority of the country's citizens.

MANDELA: This is the letter which you received on 28 June 1961? Again there was no acknowledgement or reply by the Prime Minister to this letter?

BARNARD: I don't think it is—I think it shouldn't be called a letter in the first instance, but an accumulation of threats.

Q. Whatever it is, there was no reply to it?
A. No.

On the second day of the trial, Mandela cross-examined Mr Peter Hazelhurst, a reporter on the Rand Daily Mail *and former reporter on the* Sunday Express. *He admitted under cross-examination that while White workers were free to seek work anywhere in the country and to reside near their places of employment, the African worker was made to reside in areas set aside for his occupation. He admitted that a White person was free to carry on independent trade, business, or professions anywhere in the country, while the African did not have these rights and privileges.*

Mr Hazelhurst admitted that he was aware that the whole African population was very much opposed to the pass laws. He said that 'from a humane point of view' he considered it perfectly justifiable for Africans to demand a constitution guaranteeing equal rights to them.

MANDELA: Do you know what measures the Government took to deal with this campaign? Such as mobilization throughout the country?

HAZELHURST: I can remember that the Government took certain actions, I can't remember when and where they did it.

Q. Just generally, the Government mobilized the army?
A. That is correct.

Q. There were numerous raids in the homes and offices of political opponents, people connected with the strike?
A. Yes, there were raids—in the Press reports.

Q. About ten thousand Africans were arrested shortly before the strike?
A. I can't remember when anybody was arrested, I can't remember the date now.

Q. But you remember that there were country-wide arrests before the strike?
A. I don't know whether it was before or after. I am honestly vague on that.

Q. But you remember there were arrests?
A. I think there were arrests, yes.

Q. And the type of propaganda the Government put forth

represented us as wild revolutionaries. Do you recall that?

A. It is difficult for me to answer that, it is my own opinion.

Warrant Officer Baardman, a White detective of the Bloem-fontein Special Branch, was then questioned by Mandela on the National Convention of 1909.

MANDELA: Is it true to say that the present constitution of South Africa was passed at a National Convention representing Whites only?

BAARDMAN: I don't know, I was not there.

Q. But from your knowledge?

A. I don't know, I was not there.

Q. You don't know at all?

A. No, I don't know.

Q. You want this Court to believe that, that you don't know?

A. I don't know, I was not there.

Q. Just let me put the question. You don't know that the National Convention in 1909 was a convention of Whites only?

A. I don't know, I was not there.

Q. Do you know that the Union Parliament is an all-White Parliament?

A. Yes, with representation for non-Whites.

Q. Now, I just want to ask you one or two personal questions. What standard of education have you passed?

A. Matriculation.

Q. When was this?

A. In 1932.

Q. In what medium did you write it?

A. In my mother tongue. (*Here the witness meant Afrikaans.*)

Q. I notice you are very proud of this?

A. I am.

Q. You know of course that in this country we have no language rights as Africans?

A. I don't agree with you.

Q. None of our languages is an official language, for example. Would you agree with that?

A. They are perhaps not in the Statute Book as official

languages, but no one forbids you from using your own language.

Q. Will you answer the question? Is it true that in this country there are only two official languages, and they are English and Afrikaans?

A. I agree entirely. By name they are the two official languages, but no one has ever forbidden you to use your own language.

Q. Is it true that there are only two official languages in this country, that is English and Afrikaans?

A. To please you that is so.

Q. Is it true that the Afrikaner people in this country have fought for equality of English and Afrikaans? There was a time, for example, when Afrikaans was not the official language in the history of the various colonies, like the Cape?

A. Yes, I agree with you entirely. Constitutionally, the Afrikaner did fight for his language but not through agitators.

One of several police witnesses called by the State from the Transkie admitted under cross-examination that he did not know how many Africans had been killed in his area since the state of emergency had been declared. He admitted, however, that a few hundreds had been arrested. Possibly twenty had been sentenced to death. He did not admit that a large number of people were still in detention, or that the Government had been forced to impose the state of emergency because it did not have the support of the people.

MANDELA: Perhaps there is a point on which you can help us, on a few facts which we could not get from the previous witnesses who came from that area. Now you remember that on 30 November 1960, certain regulations were promulgated in the Transkei. In terms of these regulations—you will remember this—the Minister of Native Affairs was empowered to prohibit any person from entering or being in the Transkei or from leaving it. You remember that?

POLICE WITNESS: That is so.

Q. The same regulations laid down with certain exceptions that no meeting or gathering of more than ten Africans might be held unless with the permission of the Native Commissioner?

A. Yes.

Q. You remember that. They also provided that a Native
Commissioner, member of the police, officer or NCO of the
Defence Force, chief, or headman might order persons
present at an unlawful meeting to disperse. If such an order
was not obeyed forthwith, force might be used to exact
compliance. You remember that?

A. Yes.

Q. Now then, the regulations deal with actions deemed sub-
versive. It was also rendered an offence, (a) to make any
verbal or written statement, or to do any act which was
intended or was likely to have the effect of interfering with
the authority of the State, one of its officials, or a chief or
headman, or which contained any threat that any person
would suffer loss, violence, or inconvenience. You remember
that?

A. Yes.

Q. And (b), to organize or take part in a boycott of a meeting
convened by a State official or a chief or headman, or a
boycott against any person with the object of causing him
loss or inconvenience. You remember that?

A. Yes.

Q. (c) for an African to refuse to obey a lawful order issued by
his chief or headman, or to treat a chief or headman with
disrespect. You also remember that? And then finally, any
chief so authorized by the Minister might order any African
to move with his household and property from one place to
another within the chief's area of jurisdiction. It would be
an offence to disobey such an order. You remember all these
regulations?

A. Yes.

*The third day of the trial saw a surprise application by Mandela
for the recusal of the Magistrate. This, being the second such application, was based on fresh grounds:*

MANDELA: At the very outset I want to make application for
the recusal of Your Worship from this case. As I indicated last
Monday, I hold Your Worship in high esteem, and I do not for
one single moment doubt Your Worship's sense of fairness and

justice. I still do, as I assured Your Worship last Monday. I make this application with the greatest of respect. I have been placed in possession of information to the effect that after the adjournment yesterday, Your Worship was seen leaving the Courtroom in the company of Warrant Officer Dirker of the Special Branch, and another member of the Special Branch. As Your Worship will remember, Warrant Officer Dirker gave evidence in this case on the first day of the trial. The State Prosecutor then indicated that he would be called later, on another aspect of this case. I was then given permission by the Court to defer my cross-examination of this witness until then. The second member of the Special Branch who was in the company of Your Worship, has been seen throughout this trial assisting the State Prosecutor in presenting the case against me. Your Worship was seen entering a small blue Volkswagen car; it is believed that Your Worship sat in front, as Warrant Officer Dirker drove the car. And this other member of the Special Branch sat behind. At about ten to two Your Worship was seen returning with Warrant Officer Dirker and this other member of the Special Branch.

Now, it is not known what communication passed between Your Worship and Warrant Officer Dirker and this other member of the Special Branch. I, as an accused, was not there, and was not represented. Now, these facts have created an impression in my mind that the Court has associated itself with the State case. I am left with the substantial fear that justice is being administered in a secret manner. It is an elementary rule of justice that a judicial officer should not communicate or associate in any manner whatsoever with a party to those proceedings. I submit that Your Worship should not have acted in this fashion, and I must therefore ask Your Worship to recuse yourself from this case.

THE MAGISTRATE: I can only say this, that it is not for me here to give you any reasons. I can assure you, as I here now do, that I did not communicate with these two gentlemen, and your application is refused.

A large number of witnesses, all policemen and Special Branch detectives, followed. One of these was an Indian member of the

Special Branch, Abdul Moolla, who was cross-examined on the effects of the Group Areas Act on the Indian community in particular.

MANDELA: You know about the Group Areas Act?

MOOLLA: I do.

Q. You know that it is intended to set certain areas for occupation by the various population groups in the country?

A. Yes, I do know.

Q. And you know that it has aroused a great deal of feeling and opposition from the Indian community in this country?

A. Well, not that I know of. I think that most of the Indians are satisfied with it.

Q. Is this a sincere opinion?

A. That is my sincere opinion, from people that I have met.

Q. And are you aware of the attitude of the South African Indian Congress, about the Group Areas?

A. Yes.

Q. What is the attitude of the South African Indian Congress?

A. The South African Indian Congress is against it.

Q. And the attitude of the Transvaal Indian Congress?

A. Also.

Q. They are against it?

A. Yes.

Q. And the Transvaal Indian Youth Congress?

A. Also.

Q. The Cape Indian Assembly, also against it?

A. Yes. Well, the Cape Indian Assembly I do not know about.

Q. Well, you can take it from me that it is against it. Now, of course, if the Group Areas Act is carried out in its present form, it means that a large number of Indian merchants would lose their trading rights in areas which have been declared White Areas?

A. That is right.

Q. And a large number of members of the Indian community who are living at the present moment in areas which might or have been declared as White Areas, would have to leave those homes, and have to go to where they are to be stationed?

A. I think they will be better off than where . . .

Q. Answer the question. You know that?

A. Yes, I know that.

Q. You say that the Indian merchant class in this country, who are going to lose their business rights, are happy about it?

A. Well, not all.

Q. Not all. And you are saying that those members of the Indian community who are going to be driven away from the areas where they are living at present would be happy to do so?

A. Yes they would be.

MANDELA: Well, Mr Moolla, I want to leave it at that, but just to say that you have lost your soul.

On the fourth day of the trial the Prosecution formally closed its case and the Prosecutor addressed the Court, pleading that the Court should find Mandela guilty of inciting persons in three listed categories to protest against the Republic of South Africa Constitution Act of 1961. The three categories of persons were:

(a) *employees in essential services, who are not allowed to strike;*

(b) *African mineworkers for whom it is unlawful to desert or absent themselves from employment without lawful cause; and*

(c) *servants in general, other than agricultural labourers, for whom it is unlawful to absent themselves from their masters' premises.*

The Prosecutor also asked the Court to find Mandela guilty on the second charge, that is, for leaving the Republic of South Africa without being in possession of a valid permit or passport.

The Prosecutor wound up his address to the Court and the Magistrate asked if the accused had anything to say.

MANDELA: Your Worship, I submit that I am guilty of no crimes.

MAGISTRATE: Is that all you have to say?

MANDELA: Your Worship, with respect, if I had something more to say, I would have said it.

Judgement was reserved until 7 November 1962.

Then followed Mandela's address to Court before sentence:

I AM charged with inciting people to commit an offence by way of protest against the law, a law which neither I nor any of my people had any say in preparing. The law against which the protest was directed is the law which established a Republic in the Union of South Africa. I am also charged with leaving the country without a passport. This Court has found that I am guilty of incitement to commit an offence in opposition to this law as well as of leaving the country. But in weighing up the decision as to the sentence which is to be imposed for such an offence, the Court must take into account the question of responsibility, whether it is I who is responsible or whether, in fact, a large measure of the responsibility does not lie on the shoulders of the Government which promulgated that law, knowing that my people, who constitute the majority of the population of this country, were opposed to that law, and knowing further that every legal means of demonstrating that opposition had been closed to them by prior legislation, and by Government administrative action.

The starting point in the case against me is the holding of the conference in Pietermaritzburg on 25 and 26 March last year (1961), known as the All-In African Conference, which was called by a committee which had been established by leading people and spokesmen of the whole African population, to consider the situation which was being created by the promulgation of the Republic in the country, without consultation with us, and without our consent. That conference unanimously rejected the decision of the Government, acting only in the name of and with the agreement of the White minority of this country, to establish a Republic.

It is common knowledge that the conference decided that, in place of the unilateral proclamation of a Republic by the White minority of South Africans only, it would demand in the name of the African people the calling of a truly national convention representative of all South Africans, irrespective of their colour, Black and White, to sit amicably round a table, to debate a new constitution for South Africa, which was in essence what the Government was doing by the proclamation of a Republic, and furthermore, to press on behalf of the African people, that such new constitution should differ from the constitution of the proposed South African Republic by guaranteeing democratic rights on a basis of full equality to all South Africans of adult age. The conference had assembled, knowing full well that for a long period the present National Party Government of the Union of South Africa had refused to deal with, to discuss with, or to take into consideration the views of, the overwhelming majority of the South African population on this question. And, therefore, it was not enough for this conference just to proclaim its aim, but it was also necessary for the conference to find a means of stating that aim strongly and powerfully, despite the Government's unwilling-ness to listen.

Accordingly it was decided that should the Government fail to summon such a National Convention before 31 May 1961, all sections of the population would be called on to stage a general strike for a period of three days, both to mark our protest against the establishment of a Republic, based completely on White domination over a non-White majority, and also, in a last attempt to persuade the Government to heed our legitimate claims, and thus to avoid a period of increasing bitterness and hostility and discord in South Africa.

At that conference, an Action Council was elected, and I became its secretary. It was my duty, as secretary of the committee, to establish the machinery necessary for publicizing the decision of this conference and for directing the campaign of propaganda, publicity, and organization which would flow from it.

The Court is aware of the fact that I am an attorney by pro-fession and no doubt the question will be asked why I, as an attorney who is bound, as part of my code of behaviour, to observe the laws of the country and to respect its customs and traditions, should willingly lend myself to a campaign whose ultimate aim was to bring about a strike against the proclaimed policy of the Government of this country.

In order that the Court shall understand the frame of mind which leads me to action such as this, it is necessary for me to explain the background to my own political development and to try to make this Court aware of the factors which influenced me in deciding to act as I did.

Many years ago, when I was a boy brought up in my village in the Transkei, I listened to the elders of the tribe telling stories about the good old days, before the arrival of the White man. Then our people lived peacefully, under the democratic rule of their kings and their 'amapakati', and moved freely and confidently up and down the country without let or hindrance. Then the country was ours, in our own name and right. We occupied the land, the forests, the rivers; we extracted the mineral wealth beneath the soil and all the riches of this beautiful country. We set up and operated our own Government, we controlled our own armies and we organized our own trade and commerce. The elders would tell tales of the wars fought by our ancestors in defence of the fatherland, as well as the acts of valour performed by generals and soldiers during those epic days. The names of Dingane and Bambata, among the Zulus, of Hintsa, Makana, Ndlambe of the Amaxhosa, of Sekhukhuni and others in the north, were mentioned as the pride and glory of the entire African nation.

I hoped and vowed then that, among the treasures that life might offer me, would be the opportunity to serve my people and make my own humble contribution to their freedom struggles.

The structure and organization of early African societies in this country fascinated me very much and greatly influenced the evolution of my political outlook. The land, then the main means of production, belonged to the whole tribe, and there was no individual ownership whatsoever. There were no classes, no rich or poor and no exploitation of man by man. All men were free and equal and this was the foundation of government. Recognition of this general principle found expression in the constitution of the council, variously called Imbizo, or Pitso, or Kgotla, which governs the affairs of the tribe. The council was so completely democratic that all members of the tribe could participate in its deliberations. Chief and subject, warrior and medicine man, all took part and endeavoured to influence its decisions. It was so weighty and influential a body that no step of any importance could ever be taken by the tribe without reference to it.

There was much in such a society that was primitive and insecure and it certainly could never measure up to the demands of the present epoch. But in such a society are contained the seeds of revolutionary democracy in which none will be held in slavery or servitude, and in which poverty, want, and insecurity shall be no more. This is the inspiration which, even today, inspires me and my colleagues in our political struggle.

When I reached adult stature, I became a member of the African National Congress. That was in 1944 and I have followed its policy, supported it, and believed in its aims and outlook for eighteen years. Its policy was one which appealed to my deepest inner convictions. It sought for the unity of all Africans, over-riding tribal differences among them. It sought the acquisition of political power for Africans in the land of their birth. The African National Congress further believed that all people, irrespective of the national groups to which they may belong, and irrespective of the colour of their skins, all people whose home is South Africa and who believe in the principles of democracy and of equality of men, should be treated as Africans; that all South Africans are entitled to live a free life on the basis of fullest equality of the rights and opportunities in every field, of full democratic rights, with a direct say in the affairs of the Government.

These principles have been embodied in the Freedom Charter, which none in this country will dare challenge for its place as the most democratic programme of political principles ever enunciated by any political party or organization in this country. It was for me a matter of joy and pride to be a member of an organization which has proclaimed so democratic a policy and which campaigned for it militantly and fearlessly. The principles enumerated in the Charter have not been those of African people alone, for whom the African National Congress has always been the spokesman. Those principles have been adopted as well by the Indian people and the South African Indian Congress; by a section of the Coloured people, through the South African Coloured People's Congress, and also by a farsighted, forward-looking section of the European population, whose organization in days gone by was the South African Congress of Democrats. All these organizations, like the African National Congress, supported completely the demand for one man, one vote.

Right at the beginning of my career as an attorney I encountered difficulties imposed on me because of the colour of my skin, and further difficulty surrounding me because of my membership and support of the African National Congress. I discovered, for example, that unlike a White attorney, I could not occupy business premises in the city unless I first obtained ministerial consent in terms of the Urban Areas Act. I applied for that consent, but it was never granted. Although I subsequently obtained a permit, for a limited period, in terms of the Group Areas Act, that soon expired, and the authorities refused to renew it. They insisted that my partner, Oliver Tambo, and I should leave the city and practise in an African location at the back of beyond, miles away from where clients could reach us during working hours. This was tantamount to asking us to abandon our legal practice, to give up the legal service of our people, for which we had spent many years training. No attorney worth his salt will agree easily to do so. For some years, therefore, we continued to occupy premises in the city, illegally. The threat of prosecution and ejection hung menacingly over us throughout that period. It was an act of defiance of the law. We were aware that it was, but, nevertheless, that act had been forced on us against our wishes, and we could do no other than to choose between compliance with the law and compliance with our consciences.

In the courts where we practised we were treated courteously by many officials but we were very often discriminated against by some and treated with resentment and hostility by others. We were constantly aware that no matter how well, how correctly, how adequately we pursued our career of law, we could not become a prosecutor, or a magistrate, or a judge. We became aware of the fact that as attorneys we often dealt with officials whose competence and attainments were no higher than ours, but whose superior position was maintained and protected by a White skin.

I regarded it as a duty which I owed, not just to my people, but also to my profession, to the practice of law, and to justice for all mankind, to cry out against this discrimination which is essentially unjust and opposed to the whole basis of the attitude towards justice which is part of the tradition of legal training in this country. I believed that in taking up a stand against this injustice I was upholding the dignity of what should be an honourable profession.

Nine years ago the Transvaal Law Society applied to the Supreme Court to have my name struck off the roll because of the part I had played in a campaign initiated by the African National

Congress, a campaign for the Defiance of Unjust Laws. In the opinion of the Law Society, my activity in connection with that campaign did not conform to the standards of conduct expected from members of our honourable profession, but on this occasion the Supreme Court held that I had been within my rights as an attorney, that there was nothing dishonourable in an attorney identifying himself with his people in their struggle for political rights, even if his activities should infringe upon the laws of the country; the Supreme Court rejected the application of the Law Society.

It would not be expected that with such a verdict in my favour I should discontinue my political activities. But Your Worship may well wonder why it is that I should find it necessary to persist with such conduct, which has not only brought me the difficulties I have referred to, but which has resulted in my spending some four years on a charge before the courts, of high treason, of which I was subsequently acquitted, and of many months in jail on no charge at all, merely on the basis of the Government's dislike of my views and of my activities during the whole period of the Emergency of 1960.

Your Worship, I would say that the whole life of any thinking African in this country drives him continuously to a conflict between his conscience on the one hand and the law on the other. This is not a conflict peculiar to this country. The conflict arises for men of conscience, for men who think and who feel deeply in every country. Recently in Britain, a peer of the realm, Earl Russell, probably the most respected philosopher of the Western world, was sentenced, convicted for precisely the type of activities for which I stand before you today, for following his conscience in defiance of the law, as a protest against a nuclear weapons policy being followed by his own Government. For him, his duty to the public, his belief in the morality of the essential rightness of the cause for which he stood, rose superior to this high respect for the law. He could not do other than to oppose the law and to suffer the consequences for it. Nor can I. Nor can many Africans in this country. The law as it is applied, the law as it has been developed over a long period of history, and especially the law as it is written and designed by the Nationalist Government, is a law which, in our view, *is immoral, unjust, and intolerable.* Our consciences dictate that we must protest against it, that we must oppose it, and that we must attempt to alter it.

Always we have been conscious of our obligations as citizens to avoid breaches of the law, where such breaches can be avoided, to prevent a clash between the authorities and our people, where such clash can be prevented, but nevertheless, we have been driven to speak up for what we believe is right, and to work for it and to try and bring about changes which will satisfy our human conscience.

Throughout its fifty years of existence the African National Congress, for instance, has done everything possible to bring its demands to the attention of successive South African Governments. It has sought at all times peaceful solutions for all the country's ills and problems. The history of the ANC is filled with instances where deputations were sent to South African Governments either on specific issues or on the general political demands of our people. I do not wish to burden Your Worship by enunciating the occasions when such deputations were sent; all that I wish to indicate at this stage is that, in addition to the efforts made by former presidents of the ANC, when Mr Strijdom became Prime Minister of this country, my leader, Chief A. J. Lutuli, then President of our organization, made yet another effort to persuade this Government to consider and to heed our point of view. In his letter to the Prime Minister at the time, Chief Lutuli exhaustively reviewed the country's relations and its dangers, and expressed the view that a meeting between the Government and African leaders had become necessary and urgent.

This statesmanlike and correct behaviour on the part of the leader of the majority of the South African population did not find an appropriate answer from the leader of the South African Government. The standard of behaviour of the South African Government towards my people and its aspirations has not always been what it should have been, and is not always the standard which is to be expected in serious high-level dealings between civilized peoples. Chief Lutuli's letter was not even favoured with the courtesy of an acknowledgement from the Prime Minister's office.

This experience was repeated after the Pietermaritzburg conference, when I, as Secretary of the Action Council, elected at that

conference, addressed a letter to the Prime Minister, Dr Verwoerd, informing him of the resolution which had been taken, and
calling on him to initiate steps for the convening of such a national
convention as we suggested, before the date specified in the
resolution. In a civilized country one would be outraged by the
failure of the head of Government even to acknowledge receipt of
a letter, or to consider such a reasonable request put to him by a
broadly representative collection of important personalities and
leaders of the most important community of the country. Once
again, Government standards in dealing with my people fell below
what the civilized world would expect. No reply, no response whatsoever, was received to our letter, no indication was even given that
it had received any consideration whatsoever. Here we, the African
people, and especially we of the National Action Council, who had
been entrusted with the tremendous responsibility of safeguarding
the interests of the African people, were faced with this conflict
between the law and our conscience. In the face of the complete
failure of the Government to heed, to consider, or even to respond
to our seriously proposed objections and our solutions to the
forthcoming Republic, what were we to do? Were we to allow
the law which states that you shall not commit an offence by
way of protest, to take its course and thus betray our conscience
and our belief? Were we to uphold our conscience and our beliefs
to strive for what we believe is right, not just for us, but for all the
people who live in this country, both the present generation and
for generations to come, and thus transgress against the law? This
is the dilemma which faced us and in such a dilemma, men of
honesty, men of purpose, and men of public morality and of
conscience can only have one answer. They must follow the
dictates of their conscience irrespective of the consequences which
might overtake them for it. We of the Action Council, and I
particularly as Secretary, followed my conscience.

IF I HAD MY TIME OVER I WOULD DO THE SAME AGAIN,
SO WOULD ANY MAN WHO DARES CALL HIMSELF A MAN.
We went ahead with our campaign as instructed by the conference
and in accordance with its decisions.

The issue that sharply divided White South Africans during
the referendum for a Republic did not interest us. It formed no
part in our campaign. Continued association with the British

monarchy on the one hand, or the establishment of a Boer Republic on the other—this was the crucial issue in so far as the White population was concerned and as it was put to them in the referendum. We are neither monarchists nor admirers of a Voortrekker type of republic. We believe that we were inspired by aspirations more worthy than either of the groups who took part in the campaign on these. We were inspired by the idea of bringing into being a democratic republic where all South Africans will enjoy human rights without the slightest discrimination; where African and non-African would be able to live together in peace, sharing a common nationality and a common loyalty to this country, which is our homeland. For these reasons we were opposed to the type of republic proposed by the Nationalist Party Government, just as we have been opposed previously to the constitutional basis of the Union of South Africa as a part of the British Empire. We were not prepared to accept, at a time when constitutional changes were being made, that these constitutional changes should not affect the real basis of a South African constitution, White supremacy and White domination, the very basis which has brought South Africa and its constitution into contempt and disrepute throughout the world.

I wish now to deal with the campaign itself, with the character of the campaign, and with the course of events which followed our decision. From the beginning our campaign was a campaign designed to call on people as a last extreme, if all else failed, if all discussions failed to materialize, if the Government showed no sign of taking any steps to attempt, either to treat with us or to meet our demands peacefully, to *strike*, that is to stay away from work, and so to bring economic pressure to bear. There was never any intention that our demonstrations, at that stage, go further than that. In all our statements, both those which are before the Court, and those which are not before the Court, we made it clear that that strike would be a peaceful protest, in which people were asked to remain in their homes. It was our intention that the demonstration should go through peacefully and peaceably, without clash and conflict, as such demonstrations do in every civilized country.

Nevertheless, around that campaign and our preparations for that campaign was created the atmosphere for civil war and revolution. I would say deliberately created. Deliberately created, not by us, Your Worship, but by the Government, which set out, from the beginning of this campaign, not to treat with us, not to heed us, nor to talk to us, but rather to present us as wild, dangerous revolutionaries, intent on disorder and riot, incapable of being dealt with in any way save by mustering an overwhelming force against us and the implementation of every possible forcible means, legal and illegal, to suppress us. The Government behaved in a way no civilized government should dare behave when faced with a peaceful, disciplined, sensible, and democratic expression of the views of its own population. It ordered the mobilization of its armed forces to attempt to cow and terrorize our peaceful protest. It arrested people known to be active in African politics and in support of African demands for democratic rights, passed special laws enabling it to hold them without trial for twelve days instead of the forty-eight hours which had been customary before, and hold them, the majority of them, never to be charged before the courts, but to be released after the date for the strike had passed. If there was a danger during this period that violence would result from the situation in the country, then the possibility was of the Government's making. THEY SET THE SCENE FOR VIOLENCE BY RELYING EXCLUSIVELY ON VIOLENCE WITH WHICH TO ANSWER OUR PEOPLE AND THEIR DEMANDS. The counter-measures which they took clearly reflected growing uneasiness on their part, which grew out of the knowledge that their policy did not enjoy the support of the majority of the people, while ours did. It was clear that the Government was attempting to combat the intensity of our campaign by a reign of terror. At the time the newspapers suggested the strike was a failure and it was said that we did not enjoy the support of the people. I deny that. I deny it and I will continue to deny it as long as this Government is not prepared to put to the test the question of the opinion of the African people by consulting them in a democratic way. In any event the evidence in this case has shown that it was a substantial success. Our campaign was an intensive campaign and met with tremendous and overwhelming response from the population. In the end, if a strike did not materialize on the scale on which it had been hoped it would, it was not because the people were not willing, but because the overwhelming strength, violence, and force of the Government's attack against our campaign had for the time being achieved its aim of forcing us into submission against our wishes and against our conscience.

I wish again to return to the question of why people like me, knowing all this, knowing in advance that this Government is incapable of progressive democratic moves, so far as our people are concerned, knowing that this Government is incapable of reacting towards us in any way other than by the use of over-whelming brute force, why I, and people like me, nevertheless, decide to go ahead to do what we must. We have been conditioned to our attitudes by the history which is not of our making. We have been conditioned by the history of White governments in this country to accept the fact that Africans, when they make their demands strongly and powerfully enough to have some chance of success, will be met by force and terror on the part of the Government. This is not something we have taught the African people, this is something the African people have learned from their own bitter experience. We learned it from each successive government. We learned it from the Government of General Smuts at the time of two massacres of our people: the 1921 massacre in Bulhoek when more than 100 men, women, and children were killed, and from the 1923 massacre—the Bondelswar massacre in South-West Africa, in which some 200 Africans were killed. We have continued to learn it from every successive Government.

GOVERNMENT VIOLENCE CAN DO ONLY ONE THING AND THAT IS TO BREED COUNTER-VIOLENCE. WE HAVE WARNED REPEATEDLY THAT THE GOVERNMENT, BY RESORTING CON-TINUALLY TO VIOLENCE, WILL BREED, IN THIS COUNTRY, COUNTER-VIOLENCE AMONGST THE PEOPLE, TILL ULTI-MATELY, IF THERE IS NO DAWNING OF SANITY ON THE PART OF THE GOVERNMENT—ULTIMATELY, THE DISPUTE BE-TWEEN THE GOVERNMENT AND MY PEOPLE WILL FINISH UP BY BEING SETTLED IN VIOLENCE AND BY FORCE. Already there are indications in this country that people, my people, Africans, are turning to deliberate acts of violence and of force against the Government, in order to persuade the Government, in the only language which this Government shows, by its own behaviour, that it understands.

Elsewhere in the world, a court would say to me. 'You should have made representations to the Government.' This Court, I am confident, will not say so. Representations have been made, by people who have gone before me, time and time again. Representations were made in this case by me; I do not want again to repeat the experience of those representations. The Court cannot expect a respect for the processes of representation and negotiation to grow amongst the African people, when the Government shows every day, by its conduct, that it despises such processes and frowns upon them and will not indulge in them. Nor will the Court, I believe, say that, under the circumstances, my people are condemned forever to say nothing and to do nothing. If this Court says that, or believes it, I think it is mistaken and deceiving itself. Men are not capable of doing nothing, of saying nothing, of not reacting to injustice, of not protesting against oppression, of not striving for the good society and the good life in the ways they see it. Nor will they do so in this country.

Perhaps the Court will say that despite our human rights to protest, to object, to make ourselves heard, we should stay within the letter of the law. I would say, Sir, that it is the Government, its administration of the law, which brings the law into such contempt and disrepute that one is no longer concerned in this country to stay within the letter of the law. I will illustrate this from my own experience. The Government has used the process of law to handicap me, in my personal life, in my career, and in my political work, in a way which is calculated, in my opinion, to bring about a contempt for the law. In December 1952 I was issued with an order by the Government, not as the result of a trial before a court and a conviction, but as a result of prejudice, or perhaps Star Chamber procedure behind closed doors in the halls of Government. In terms of that order I was confined to the Magisterial district of Johannesburg for six months and, at the same time, I was prohibited from attending gatherings for a similar period. That order expired in June 1953 and three months thereafter, again without any hearing, without any attempt to hear my side of the case, without facing me with charges, or explanations, both bans were renewed for a further period of two years. To these bans a third was added: I was ordered by the Minister of Justice to resign altogether from the African National Congress, and never again to become a member or to participate in its activities. Towards the end of 1955, I found myself free and able to move around once again, but not for long. In February 1956 the bans were again renewed, administratively, again without hearing, this time for five years. Again, by order of the Government, in the name of the law, I found myself restricted and isolated from my fellow men, from people who think like me and believe like me. I found myself trailed by officers of the Security Branch of the Police Force wherever I went. In short I found myself treated as a criminal—an unconvicted criminal. I was not allowed to pick my company, to frequent the company of men, to participate in their political activities, to join their organizations. I was not free from constant police surveillance. I was made, by the law, a criminal, not because of what I had done, but because of what I stood for, because of what I thought, because of my conscience. Can it be any wonder to anybody that such conditions make a man an outlaw of society? Can it be wondered that such a man, having been outlawed by the Government, should be prepared to lead the life of an outlaw, as I have led for some months, according to the evidence before this Court?

It has not been easy for me during the past period to separate myself from my wife and children, to say goodbye to the good old days when, at the end of a strenuous day at an office, I could look forward to joining my family at the dinner-table, and instead to take up the life of a man hunted continuously by the police, living separated from those who are closest to me, in my own country, facing continually the hazards of detection and of arrest. This has been a life infinitely more difficult than serving a prison sentence. No man in his right senses would voluntarily choose such a life in preference to the one of normal, family, social life which exists in every civilized community.

BUT THERE COMES A TIME, AS IT CAME IN MY LIFE, WHEN A MAN IS DENIED THE RIGHT TO LIVE A NORMAL LIFE, WHEN HE CAN ONLY LIVE THE LIFE OF AN OUTLAW BECAUSE THE GOVERNMENT HAS SO DECREED TO USE THE LAW TO IMPOSE A STATE OF OUTLAWRY UPON HIM. I was driven to this situation, and I do not regret having taken the decisions that I did take. Other people will be driven in the same way in this country, by this same very force of police persecution and of administrative action by the Government, to follow my course, of that I am certain. The decision that I should continue to carry out the decisions of the Pietermaritzburg conference, despite police persecution all the time, was not my decision alone. It was a decision reached by me, in consultation with those who were entrusted with the leadership of the campaign and its fulfilment. It was clear to us then, in the early periods of the campaign, when the Government was busy whipping up an atmosphere of hysteria as the prelude to violence, that the views of the African people would not be heard, would not find expression, unless attempts were made deliberately by those of us entrusted with the task of carrying through the strike call to keep away from the illegal, unlawful attacks of the Special Branch, the unlawful detention of people for twelve days without trial, and unlawful and illegal intervention by the police and the Government forces in legitimate political activity of the population. I was, at the time of the Pietermaritzburg conference, free from bans for a short time, and a time which I had no reason to expect would prolong itself for very long. Had I remained in my normal surroundings, carrying on my normal life, I would have again been forced by Government action to a position of an outlaw. That I was not prepared to do while the commands of the Pietermaritzburg conference to me remained unfulfilled. New situations require new tactics. The situation, which was not our making, which followed the Pietermaritzburg conference required the tactics which I adopted, I believe, correctly.

A lot has been written since the Pietermaritzburg conference, and even more since my arrest, much of which is flattering to my pride and dear to my heart, but much of which is mistaken and incorrect. It has been suggested that the advances, the articulateness of our people, the successes which they are achieving here, and the recognition which they are winning both here and abroad are in some way the result of my work. I must place on record my belief that I have been only one in a large army of people, to all of whom the credit for any success of achievement is due. Advance and progress is not the result of my work alone, but of the collective work of my colleagues and I, both here and abroad. I have been fortunate throughout my political life to work together with colleagues whose abilities and contributions to the cause of my people's freedom have been greater and better than my own, people who have been loved and respected by the African population generally as a result of the dedicated way in which they have fought for freedom and for peace and justice in this country. It distresses me to read reports that my arrest has been instigated by some of my colleagues for some sinister purposes of their own. Nothing could be further from the truth. I dismiss these suggestions as the sensational inventions of unscrupulous journalists. People who stoop to such unscrupulous manoeuvres as the betrayal of their own comrades have no place in the good fight which I have fought for the freedom of the African people, which my colleagues continue to fight without me today. Not just I alone, but all of us are willing to pay the penalties which we may have to pay, which I may have to pay for having followed my conscience in pursuit of what I believe is right. So are we all. Many people in this country have paid the price before me, and many will pay the price after me.

I do not believe, Your Worship, that this Court in inflicting penalties on me for the crimes for which I am convicted, should be moved by the belief that penalties deter men from the course that they believe is right. History shows that penalties do not deter men when their conscience is aroused, nor will they deter my people or the colleagues with whom I have worked before.

I am prepared to pay the penalty even though I know how bitter and desperate is the situation of an African in the prisons of this country. I have been in these prisons and I know how gross is the discrimination, even behind the prison walls, against Africans, how much worse is the treatment meted out to African prisoners than that accorded to Whites. Nevertheless, these considerations do not sway me from the path that I have taken, nor will they sway others like me. For to men, freedom in their own land is the pinnacle of their ambitions, from which nothing can turn men of conviction aside. More powerful than my fear of the dreadful conditions to which I might be subjected is my hatred for the dreadful conditions to which my people are subjected outside prison throughout this country.

I hate the practice of race discrimination, and in my hatred I am sustained by the fact that the overwhelming majority of mankind hate it equally. I hate the systematic inculcation of children with colour prejudice and I am sustained in that hatred by the fact that the overwhelming majority of mankind, here and abroad, are with me in that. I hate the racial arrogance which decrees that the good things of life shall be retained as the exclusive right of a minority of the population, and which reduces the majority of the population to a position of subservience and inferiority, and maintains them as voteless chattels to work where they are told and behave as they are told by the ruling minority. I am sustained in that hatred by the fact that the overwhelming majority of mankind both in this country and abroad are with me.

Nothing that this Court can do to me will change in any way that hatred in me, which can only be removed by the removal of the injustice and the inhumanity which I have sought to remove from the political, social, and economic life of this country.

Whatever sentence Your Worship sees fit to impose upon me for the crime for which I have been convicted before this Court, may it rest assured that when my sentence has been completed, I will still be moved, as men are always moved, by their consciences; I will still be moved by my dislike of the race discrimination against my people when I come out from serving my sentence, to take up again, as best I can, the struggle for the removal of those injustices until they are finally abolished once and for all.

I now wish to deal with the Second Count.

When my colleagues and I received the invitation to attend the Conference of the Pan-African Freedom Movement for East and Central Africa, it was decided that I should leave the country and join our delegation to Addis Ababa, the capital of Ethiopia, where the conference would be held. It was part of my mandate to tour Africa and make direct contact with African leaders on the continent.

I did not apply for a passport because I knew very well that it would not be granted to me. After all, the Nationalist Party Government, throughout the fourteen years of its oppressive rule, had refused permission to leave the country to many African scholars, educationalists, artists, sportsmen, and clerics, and I wished to waste none of my time by applying for a passport.

The tour of the continent made a forceful impression on me. For the first time in my life I was a free man; free from White oppression, from the idiocy of apartheid and racial arrogance, from police molestation, from humiliation and indignity. Wherever I went I was treated like a human being. I met Rashidi Kawawa, Prime Minister of Tanganyika, and Julius Nyerere. I was received by Emperor Haile Selassie, by General Abboud, President of Sudan, by Habib Bourguiba, President of Tunisia, and by Modibo Keita of the Republic of Mali.

I met Léopold Senghor, President of Senegal, Presidents Sékou Touré and Tubman, of Guinea and Liberia, respectively.

I met Ben Bella, the President of Algeria, and Colonel Boumediene, the Commander-in-Chief of the Algerian Army of National Liberation. I saw the cream and flower of the Algerian youth who had fought French imperialism and whose valour had brought freedom and happiness to their country.

In London I was received by Hugh Gaitskell, Leader of the Labour Party, and by Jo Grimond, Leader of the Liberal Party, and other prominent Englishmen.

I met Prime Minister Obote of Uganda, distinguished African nationalists like Kenneth Kaunda, Oginga Odinga, Joshua Nkomo, and many others. In all these countries we were showered with hospitality, and assured of solid support for our cause.

In its efforts to keep the African people in a position of perpetual subordination, South Africa must and will fail. South Africa is out of step with the rest of the civilized world, as is shown by the resolution adopted last night by the General Assembly of the United Nations Organization which decided to impose diplomatic and economic sanctions. In the African States, I saw Black and White mingling peacefully and happily in hotels, cinemas, trading in the same areas, using the same public transport, and living in the same residential areas.

I had to return home to report to my colleagues and to share my impressions and experiences with them.

I have done my duty to my people and to South Africa. I have no doubt that posterity will pronounce that I was innocent and that the criminals that should have been brought before this Court are the members of the Verwoerd Government.

November 1962

I5

Editor's note

MANDELA was sentenced to three years' imprisonment for incitement to strike, and two years' imprisonment on the second charge of leaving South Africa without a valid permit or passport. At the close of the trial, the crowd of supporters and spectators ignored the Government ban on demonstrations and marched up the street singing 'Tshotsholoza Mandela' ('Carry on Mandela').

Mandela began to serve his five-year sentence in Pretoria Central Prison. There he spent twenty-three out of twenty-four hours in solitary confinement in his cell, sewing mailbags.

On 11 June 1963 the police raided the underground headquarters in Rivonia, a Johannesburg suburb, and arrested Walter Sisulu, Govan Mbeki, Raymond Mhlaba, Ahmed Kathrada, Dennis Goldberg, Lionel Bernstein, and others. The Rivonia trial began in October 1963 and Mandela was taken from his cell to join those in the dock facing trial for sabotage and a conspiracy to overthrow the Government by revolution and by assisting an armed invasion of South Africa by foreign troops. The leaders were joined by Elias Motsoaledi and Andrew Mlangeni, making nine accused men in all. The prosecution's key witnesses had nearly all been held for long periods in solitary detention.

Mandela opened the defence case and in his statement to Court on 20 April 1964 he said he had been one of the founders of Umkonto we Sizwe.

THE RIVONIA TRIAL

I AM the First Accused.

I hold a Bachelor's Degree in Arts and practised as an attorney in Johannesburg for a number of years in partnership with Oliver Tambo. I am a convicted prisoner serving five years for leaving the country without a permit and for inciting people to go on strike at the end of May 1961.

At the outset, I want to say that the suggestion made by the State in its opening that the struggle in South Africa is under the influence of foreigners or communists is wholly incorrect. I have done whatever I did, both as an individual and as a leader of my people, because of my experience in South Africa and my own proudly felt African background, and not because of what any outsider might have said.

In my youth in the Transkei I listened to the elders of my tribe telling stories of the old days. Amongst the tales they related to me were those of wars fought by our ancestors in defence of the fatherland. . . . I hoped then that life might offer me the opportunity to serve my people and make my own humble contribution to their freedom struggle. This is what has motivated me in all that I have done in relation to the charges made against me in this case.

Having said this, I must deal immediately and at some length with the question of violence. Some of the things so far told to the Court are true and some are untrue. I do not, however, deny that I planned sabotage. I did not plan it in a spirit of recklessness, nor because I have any love of violence. I planned it as a result of a calm and sober assessment of the political situation that had arisen after many years of tyranny, exploitation, and oppression of my people by the Whites.

I admit immediately that I was one of the persons who helped to form Umkonto we Sizwe, and that I played a prominent role in its affairs until I was arrested in August 1962.

In the statement which I am about to make I shall correct certain false impressions which have been created by State witnesses. Amongst other things, I will demonstrate that certain of the acts referred to in the evidence were not and could not have been committed by Umkonto. I will also deal with the relationship between the African National Congress and Umkonto, and with the part which I personally have played in the affairs of both organizations. I shall deal also with the part played by the Communist Party. In order to explain these matters properly I will have to explain what Umkonto set out to achieve; what methods it prescribed for the achievement of these objects, and why these methods were chosen. I will also have to explain how I became involved in the activities of these organizations.

I deny that Umkonto was responsible for a number of acts which clearly fell outside the policy of the organization, and which have been charged in the indictment against us. I do not know what justification there was for these acts, but to demonstrate that they could not have been authorized by Umkonto, I want to refer briefly to the roots and policy of the organization.

I have already mentioned that I was one of the persons who helped to form Umkonto. I, and the others who started the organization, did so for two reasons. Firstly, we believed that as a result of Government policy, violence by the African people had become inevitable, and that unless responsible leadership was given to canalize and control the feelings of our people, there would be outbreaks of terrorism which would produce an intensity of bitterness and hostility between the various races of this country which is not produced even by war. Secondly, we felt that without violence there would be no way open to the African people to succeed in their struggle against the principle of White supremacy. All lawful modes of expressing opposition to this principle had been closed by legislation, and we were placed in a position in which we had either to accept a permanent state of inferiority, or to defy the Government. We chose to defy the law. We first broke the law in a way which avoided any recourse to violence; when this form was legislated against, and then the Government resorted to a show of force to crush opposition to its policies, only then did we decide to answer violence with violence.

But the violence which we chose to adopt was not terrorism. We who formed Umkonto were all members of the African National Congress, and had behind us the ANC tradition of non-violence and negotiation as a means of solving political disputes. We believe that South Africa belonged to all the people who lived in it, and not to one group, be it Black or White. We did not want an inter-racial war, and tried to avoid it to the last minute. If the Court is in doubt about this, it will be seen that the whole history of our organization bears out what I have said, and what I will subsequently say, when I describe the tactics which Umkonto decided to adopt. I want, therefore, to say something about the African National Congress.

The African National Congress was formed in 1912 to defend the rights of the African people which had been seriously curtailed by the South Africa Act, and which were then being threatened by the Native Land Act. For thirty-seven years—that is until 1949—it adhered strictly to a constitutional struggle. It put forward demands and resolutions; it sent delegations to the Government in the belief that African grievances could be settled through peaceful discussion and that Africans could advance gradually to full political rights. But White Governments remained unmoved, and the rights of Africans became less instead of becoming greater. In the words of my leader, Chief Lutuli, who became President of the ANC in 1952, and who was later awarded the Nobel Peace Prize:

'who will deny that thirty years of my life have been spent knocking in vain, patiently, moderately, and modestly at a closed and barred door? What have been the fruits of moderation? The past thirty years have seen the greatest number of laws restricting our rights and progress, until today we have reached a stage where we have almost no rights at all.'

Even after 1949, the ANC remained determined to avoid violence. At this time, however, there was a change from the strictly constitutional means of protest which had been employed in the past. The change was embodied in a decision which was taken to protest against apartheid legislation by peaceful, but unlawful, demonstrations against certain laws. Pursuant to this policy the ANC launched the Defiance Campaign, in which I was placed in charge of volunteers. This campaign was based on the principles of passive resistance. More than 8,500 people defied apartheid laws and went to jail. Yet there was not a single instance of violence in the course of this campaign on the part of any defier. I and nineteen colleagues were convicted for the role which we played in organizing the campaign, but our sentences were suspended mainly because the Judge found that discipline and non-violence had been stressed throughout. This was the time when the volunteer section of the ANC was established, and when the word 'Amadelakufa' was first used: this was the time when the volunteers were asked to take a pledge to uphold certain principles. Evidence dealing with volunteers and their pledges has been introduced into this case, but completely out of context.

The volunteers were not, and are not, the soldiers of a Black army pledged to fight a civil war against the Whites. They were, and are, the dedicated workers who are prepared to lead campaigns initiated by the ANC to distribute leaflets; to organize strikes, or do whatever the particular campaign required. They are called volunteers because they volunteer to face the penalties of imprisonment and whipping which are now prescribed by the legislature for such acts.

During the Defiance Campaign, the Public Safety Act and the Criminal Law Amendment Act were passed. These Statutes provided harsher penalties for offences committed by way of protests against laws. Despite this, the protests continued and the ANC adhered to its policy of non-violence. In 1956, 156 leading members of the Congress Alliance, including myself, were arrested on a charge of high treason and charges under the Suppression of Communism Act. The non-violent policy of the ANC was put in issue by the State, but when the Court gave judgement some five years later, it found that the ANC did not have a policy of violence. We were acquitted on all counts, which included a count that the ANC sought to set up a communist state in place of the existing régime. The Government has always sought to label all its opponents as communists. This allegation has been repeated in the present case, but as I will show, the ANC is not, and never has been, a communist organization.

In 1960 there was the shooting at Sharpeville, which resulted in the proclamation of a state of emergency and the declaration of the ANC as an unlawful organization. My colleagues and I, after careful consideration, decided that we would not obey this decree. The African people were not part of the Government and did not make the laws by which they were governed. We believed in the words of the Universal Declaration of Human Rights, that 'the will of the people shall be the basis of authority of the Government', and for us to accept the banning was equivalent to accepting the silencing of the Africans for all time. The ANC refused to dissolve, but instead went underground. We believed it was our duty to preserve this organization which had been built up with almost fifty years of unremitting toil. I have no doubt that no self-respecting White political organization would disband itself if declared illegal by a government in which it had no say . . .

In 1960 the Government held a referendum which led to the establishment of the Republic. Africans, who constituted approximately 70 per cent of the population of South Africa, were not entitled to vote, and were not even consulted about the proposed constitutional change. All of us were apprehensive of our future under the proposed White Republic, and a resolution was taken to hold an All-In African Conference to call for a National Convention, and to organize mass demonstrations on the eve of the unwanted Republic, if the Government failed to call the Convention. The conference was attended by Africans of various political persuasions. I was the Secretary of the conference and undertook to be responsible for organizing the national stay-at-home which was subsequently called to coincide with the declaration of the Republic. As all strikes by Africans are illegal, the person organizing such a strike must avoid arrest. I was chosen to be this person, and consequently I had to leave my home and family and my practice and go into hiding to avoid arrest.

The stay-at-home, in accordance with ANC policy, was to be a peaceful demonstration. Careful instructions were given to organizers and members to avoid any recourse to violence. The Government's answer was to introduce new and harsher laws, to mobilize its armed forces, and to send saracens, armed vehicles, and soldiers into the townships in a massive show of force designed to intimidate the people. This was an indication that the Government had decided to rule by force alone, and this decision was a milestone on the road to Umkonto.

Some of this may appear irrelevant to this trial. In fact, I believe none of it is irrelevant because it will, I hope, enable the Court to appreciate the attitude eventually adopted by the various persons and bodies concerned in the National Liberation Movement. When I went to jail in 1962, the dominant idea was that loss of life should be avoided. I now know that this was still so in 1963.

I must return to June 1961. What were we, the leaders of our people, to do? Were we to give in to the show of force and the implied threat against future action, or were we to fight it and, if so, how?

We had no doubt that we had to continue the fight. Anything else would have been abject surrender. Our problem was not whether to fight, but was how to continue the fight. We of the ANC had always stood for a non-racial democracy, and we shrank from any action which might drive the races further apart than they already were. But the hard facts were that fifty years of non-violence had brought the African people nothing but more and more repressive legislation, and fewer and fewer rights. It may not be easy for this Court to understand, but it is a fact that for a long time the people had been talking of violence—of the day when they would fight the White man and win back their country—and we, the leaders of the ANC, had nevertheless always prevailed upon them to avoid violence and to pursue peaceful methods. When some of us discussed this in May and June of 1961, it could not be denied that our policy to achieve a non-racial State by non-violence had achieved nothing, and that our followers were beginning to lose confidence in this policy and were developing disturbing ideas of terrorism.

It must not be forgotten that by this time violence had, in fact, become a feature of the South African political scene. There had been violence in 1957 when the women of Zeerust were ordered to carry passes; there was violence in 1958 with the enforcement of cattle culling in Sekhukhuniland; there was violence in 1959 when the people of Cato Manor protested against pass raids; there was violence in 1960 when the Government attempted to impose Bantu Authorities in Pondoland. Thirty-nine Africans died in these disturbances. In 1961 there had been riots in Warmbaths, and all this time the Transkei had been a seething mass of unrest. Each disturbance pointed clearly to the inevitable growth among Africans of the belief that violence was the only way out—it showed that a Government which uses force to maintain its rule teaches the oppressed to use force to oppose it. Already small groups had arisen in the urban areas and were spontaneously making plans for violent forms of political struggle. There now arose a danger that these groups would adopt terrorism against Africans, as well as Whites, if not properly directed. Particularly disturbing was the type of violence engendered in places such as Zeerust, Sekhukhuniland, and Pondoland amongst Africans. It was increasingly taking the form, not of struggle against the Government—though this is what prompted it—but of civil strife amongst themselves, conducted in such a way that it could not hope to achieve anything other than a loss of life and bitterness.

At the beginning of June 1961, after a long and anxious assessment of the South African situation, I, and some colleagues, came to the conclusion that as violence in this country was inevitable, it would be unrealistic and wrong for African leaders to continue preaching peace and non-violence at a time when the Government met our peaceful demands with force.

This conclusion was not easily arrived at. It was only when all else had failed, when all channels of peaceful protest had been barred to us, that the decision was made to embark on violent forms of political struggle, and to form Umkonto we Sizwe. We did so not because we desired such a course, but solely because the Government had left us with no other choice. In the Manifesto of Umkonto published on 16 December 1961, which is Exhibit AD, we said:

'The time comes in the life of any nation when there remain only two choices—submit or fight. That time has now come to South Africa. We shall not submit and we have no choice but to hit back by all means in our power in defence of our people, our future, and our freedom.'

This was our feeling in June of 1961 when we decided to press for a change in the policy of the National Liberation Movement. I can only say that I felt morally obliged to do what I did.

We who had taken this decision started to consult leaders of various organizations, including the ANC. I will not say whom we spoke to, or what they said, but I wish to deal with the role of the African National Congress in this phase of the struggle, and with the policy and objectives of Umkonto we Sizwe.

As far as the ANC was concerned, it formed a clear view which can be summarized as follows:

(a) It was a mass political organization with a political function to fulfil. Its members had joined on the express policy of non-violence.

(b) Because of all this, it could not and would not undertake violence. This must be stressed. One cannot turn such a body into the small, closely knit organization required for sabotage. Nor would this be politically correct, because it would result in members ceasing to carry out this essential activity; political propaganda and organization. Nor was it permissible to change the whole nature of the organization.

(c) On the other hand, in view of this situation I have described, the ANC was prepared to depart from its fifty-year-old policy of non-violence to this extent that it would no longer disapprove of properly controlled violence. Hence members who undertook such activity would not be subject to disciplinary action by the ANC.

I say 'properly controlled violence' because I made it clear that if I formed the organization I would at all times subject it to the political guidance of the ANC and would not undertake any different form of activity from that contemplated without the consent of the ANC. And I shall now tell the Court how that form of violence came to be determined.

As a result of this decision, Umkonto was formed in November 1961. When we took this decision, and subsequently formulated our plans, the ANC heritage of non-violence and racial harmony was very much with us. We felt that the country was drifting towards a civil war in which Blacks and Whites would fight each other. We viewed the situation with alarm. Civil war could mean the destruction of what the ANC stood for; with civil war, racial peace would be more difficult than ever to achieve. We already have examples in South African history of the results of war. It has taken more than fifty years for the scars of the South African War to disappear. How much longer would it take to eradicate the scars of inter-racial civil war, which could not be fought without a great loss of life on both sides?

The avoidance of civil war had dominated our thinking for many years, but when we decided to adopt violence as part of our policy, we realized that we might one day have to face the prospect of such a war. This had to be taken into account in formulating our plans. We required a plan which was flexible and which permitted us to act in accordance with the needs of the times; above all, the plan had to be one which recognized civil war as the last resort, and left the decision on this question to the future. We did not want to be committed to civil war, but we wanted to be ready if it became inevitable.

Four forms of violence were possible. There is sabotage, there is guerrilla warfare, there is terrorism, and there is open revolution. We chose to adopt the first method and to exhaust it before taking any other decision.

In the light of our political background the choice was a logical one. Sabotage did not involve loss of life, and it offered the best hope for future race relations. Bitterness would be kept to a minimum and, if the policy bore fruit, democratic government could become a reality. This is what we felt at the time, and this is what we said in our Manifesto (Exhibit AD):

'We of Umkonto We Sizwe have always sought to achieve liberation without bloodshed and civil clash. We hope, even at this late hour, that our first actions will awaken everyone to a realization of the disastrous situation to which the Nationalist policy is leading. We hope that we will bring the Government and its supporters to their senses before it is too late, so that both the Government and its policies can be changed before matters reach the desperate stage of civil war.'

The initial plan was based on a careful analysis of the political and economic situation of our country. We believed that South Africa depended to a large extent on foreign capital and foreign trade. We felt that planned destruction of power plants, and interference with rail and telephone communications, would tend to scare away capital from the country, make it more difficult for goods from the industrial areas to reach the seaports on schedule, and would in the long run be a heavy drain on the economic life of the country, thus compelling the voters of the country to reconsider their position.

Attacks on the economic life lines of the country were to be linked with sabotage on Government buildings and other symbols of apartheid. These attacks would serve as a source of inspiration to our people. In addition, they would provide an outlet for those people who were urging the adoption of violent methods and would enable us to give concrete proof to our followers that we had adopted a stronger line and were fighting back against Government violence.

In addition, if mass action were successfully organized, and mass reprisals taken, we felt that sympathy for our cause would be roused in other countries, and that greater pressure would be brought to bear on the South African Government.

This then was the plan. Umkonto was to perform sabotage, and strict instructions were given to its members right from the start, that on no account were they to injure or kill people in planning or carrying out operations. These instructions have been referred to in the evidence of 'Mr X' and 'Mr Z'.

The affairs of the Umkonto were controlled and directed by a National High Command, which had powers of co-option and which could, and did, appoint Regional Commands. The High Command was the body which determined tactics and targets and was in charge of training and finance. Under the High Command there were Regional Commands which were responsible for the direction of the local sabotage groups. Within the framework of the policy laid down by the National High Command, the Regional Commands had authority to select the targets to be attacked. They had no authority to go beyond the prescribed framework and thus had no authority to embark upon acts which endangered life, or which did not fit into the overall plan of sabotage. For instance, Umkonto members were forbidden ever to go armed into operation. Incidentally, the terms High Command and Regional Command were an importation from the Jewish nation underground organization Irgun Zvai Leumi, which operated in Israel between 1944 and 1948.

Umkonto had its first operation on 16 December 1961, when Government buildings in Johannesburg, Port Elizabeth, and Durban were attacked. The selection of targets is proof of the policy to which I have referred. Had we intended to attack life we would have selected targets where people congregated and not empty buildings and power stations. The sabotage which was committed before 16 December 1961 was the work of isolated groups and had no connection whatever with Umkonto. In fact, some of these and a number of later acts were claimed by other organizations.

The Manifesto of Umkonto was issued on the day that operations commenced. The response to our actions and Manifesto among the White population was characteristically violent. The Government threatened to take strong action, and called upon its supporters to stand firm and to ignore the demands of the Africans. The Whites failed to respond by suggesting change; they responded to our call by suggesting the laager.

In contrast, the response of the Africans was one of encouragement. Suddenly there was hope again. Things were happening. People in the townships became eager for political news. A great deal of enthusiasm was generated by the initial successes, and people began to speculate on how soon freedom would be obtained.

But we in Umkonto weighed up the White response with anxiety. The lines were being drawn. The Whites and Blacks were moving into separate camps, and the prospects of avoiding a civil war were made less. The White newspapers carried reports that sabotage would be punished by death. If this was so, how could we continue to keep Africans away from terrorism?

Already scores of Africans had died as a result of racial friction. In 1920 when the famous leader, Masabala, was held in Port Elizabeth jail, twenty-four of a group of Africans who had gathered to demand his release were killed by the police and White civilians. In 1921, more than one hundred Africans died in the Bulhoek affair. In 1924 over two hundred Africans were killed when the Administrator of South-West Africa led a force against a group which had rebelled against the imposition of dog tax. On 1 May 1950, eighteen Africans died as a result of police shootings during the strike. On 21 March 1960, sixty-nine unarmed Africans died at Sharpeville.

How many more Sharpevilles would there be in the history of our country? And how many more Sharpevilles could the country stand without violence and terror becoming the order of the day? And what would happen to our people when that stage was reached? In the long run we felt certain we must succeed, but at what cost to ourselves and the rest of the country? And if this happened, how could Black and White ever live together again in peace and harmony? These were the problems that faced us, and these were our decisions.

Experience convinced us that rebellion would offer the Government limitless opportunities for the indiscriminate slaughter of our people. But it was precisely because the soil of South Africa is already drenched with the blood of innocent Africans that we felt it our duty to make preparations as a long-term undertaking to use force in order to defend ourselves against force. If war were inevitable, we wanted the fight to be conducted on terms most favourable to our people. The fight which held out prospects best for us and the least risk of life to both sides was guerrilla warfare. We decided, therefore, in our preparations for the future, to make provision for the possibility of guerrilla warfare.

All Whites undergo compulsory military training, but no such training was given to Africans. It was in our view essential to build up a nucleus of trained men who would be able to provide the leadership which would be required if guerrilla warfare started. We had to prepare for such a situation before it became too late to make proper preparations. It was also necessary to build up a nucleus of men trained in civil administration and other professions, so that Africans would be equipped to participate in the government of this country as soon as they were allowed to do so.

At this stage it was decided that I should attend the Conference of the Pan-African Freedom Movement for Central, East, and Southern Africa, which was to be held early in 1962 in Addis Ababa, and, because of our need for preparation, it was also decided that, after the conference, I would undertake a tour of the African States with a view to obtaining facilities for the training of soldiers, and that I would also solicit scholarships for the higher education of matriculated Africans. Training in both fields would be necessary, even if changes came about by peaceful means. Administrators would be necessary who would be willing and able to administer a non-racial State and so would men be necessary to control the army and police force of such a State.

It was on this note that I left South Africa to proceed to Addis Ababa as a delegate of the ANC. My tour was a success. Wherever I went I met sympathy for our cause and promises of help. All Africa was united against the stand of White South Africa, and even in London I was received with great sympathy by political leaders, such as Mr Gaitskell and Mr Grimond. In Africa I was promised support by such men as Julius Nyerere, now President of Tanganyika; Mr Kawawa, then Prime Minister of Tanganyika; Emperor Haile Selassie of Ethiopia; General Abboud, President of the Sudan; Habib Bourguiba, President of Tunisia; Ben Bella, now President of Algeria; Modibo Keita, President of Mali; Léopold Senghor, President of Senegal; Sékou Touré, President of Guinea; President Tubman of Liberia; and Milton Obote, Prime Minister of Uganda. It was Ben Bella who invited me to visit Oujda, the Headquarters of the Algerian Army of National Liberation, the visit which is described in my diary, one of the Exhibits.

I started to make a study of the art of war and revolution and, whilst abroad, underwent a course in military training. If there was to be guerrilla warfare, I wanted to be able to stand and fight with my people and to share the hazards of war with them. Notes of lectures which I received in Algeria are contained in Exhibit 16, produced in evidence. Summaries of books on guerrilla warfare and military strategy have also been produced. I have already admitted that these documents are in my writing, and I acknowledge that I made these studies to equip myself for the role which I might have to play if the struggle drifted into guerrilla warfare. I approached this question as every African Nationalist should do. I was completely objective. The Court will see that I attempted to examine all types of authority on the subject—from the East and from the West, going back to the classic work of Clausewitz, and covering such a variety as Mao Tse Tung and Che Guevara on the one hand, and the writings on the Anglo-Boer War on the other. Of course, these notes are merely summaries of the books I read and do not contain my personal views.

I also made arrangements for our recruits to undergo military training. But here it was impossible to organize any scheme without the cooperation of the ANC offices in Africa. I consequently obtained the permission of the ANC in South Africa to do this. To this extent then there was a departure from the original decision of the ANC, but it applied outside South Africa only. The first batch of recruits actually arrived in Tanganyika when I was passing through that country on my way back to South Africa.

I returned to South Africa and reported to my colleagues on the results of my trip. On my return I found that there had been little alteration in the political scene save that the threat of a death penalty for sabotage had now become a fact. The attitude of my colleagues in Umkonto was much the same as it had been before I left. They were feeling their way cautiously and felt that it would be a long time before the possibilities of sabotage were exhausted. In fact, the view was expressed by some that the training of recruits was premature. This is recorded by me in the document, which is Exhibit R. 14. After a full discussion, however, it was decided to go ahead with the plans for military training because of the fact that it would take many years to build up a sufficient nucleus of trained soldiers to start a guerrilla campaign, and whatever happened the training would be of value. . . .

I wish to turn now to certain general allegations made in this case by the State. But before doing so, I wish to revert to certain occurrences said by witnesses to have happened in Port Elizabeth and East London. I am referring to the bombing of private houses of pro-Government persons during September, October, and November 1962. I do not know what justification there was for these acts, nor what provocation had been given. But if what I have said already is accepted, then it is clear that these acts had nothing to do with the carrying out of the policy of Umkonto.

One of the chief allegations in the indictment is that the ANC was a party to a general conspiracy to commit sabotage. I have already explained why this is incorrect but how, externally, there was a departure from the original principle laid down by the ANC. There has, of course, been overlapping of functions internally as well, because there is a difference between a resolution adopted in the atmosphere of a committee room and the concrete difficulties that arise in the field of practical activity. At a later stage the position was further affected by bannings and house arrests, and by persons leaving the country to take up political work abroad. This led to individuals having to do work in different capacities. But though this may have blurred the distinction between Umkonto and the ANC, it by no means abolished that distinction. Great care was taken to keep the activities of the two organizations in South Africa distinct. The ANC remained a mass political body of Africans only carrying on the type of political work they had conducted prior to 1961. Umkonto remained a small organization recruiting its members from different races and organizations and trying to achieve its own particular object. The fact that members of Umkonto were recruited from the ANC, and the fact that persons served both organizations, like Solomon Mbanjwa, did not, in our view, change the nature of the ANC or give it a policy of violence. This overlapping of officers, however, was more the exception than the rule. This is why persons such as 'Mr X' and 'Mr Z', who were on the Regional Command of their respective areas, did not participate in any of the ANC committees or activities, and why people such as Mr Bennett Mashiyana and Mr Reginald Ndubi did not hear of sabotage at their ANC meetings.

Another of the allegations in the indictment is that Rivonia was the headquarters of Umkonto. This is not true of the time when I was there. I was told, of course, and knew that certain of the activities of the Communist Party were carried on there. But this is no reason (as I shall presently explain) why I should not use the place.

I came there in the following manner:

(a) As already indicated, early in April 1961 I went underground to organize the May general strike. My work entailed travelling throughout the country, living now in African townships, then in country villages and again in cities.

    During the second half of the year I started visiting the Parktown home of Arthur Goldreich, where I used to meet my family privately. Although I had no direct political association with him, I had known Arthur Goldreich socially since 1958.

(b) In October, Arthur Goldreich informed me that he was moving out of town and offered me a hiding place there. A few days thereafter, he arranged for Michael Harmel to take me to Rivonia. I naturally found Rivonia an ideal place for the man who lived the life of an outlaw. Up to that time I had been compelled to live indoors during the daytime and could only venture out under cover of darkness. But at Liliesleaf I could live differently and work far more efficiently.

(c) For obvious reasons, I had to disguise myself and I assumed the fictitious name of David. In December, Arthur Goldreich and his family moved in. I stayed there until I went abroad on 11 January 1962. As already indicated, I returned in July 1962 and was arrested in Natal on 5 August.

(d) Up to the time of my arrest, Liliesleaf farm was the headquarters of neither the African National Congress nor Umkonto. With the exception of myself, none of the officials or members of these bodies lived there, no meetings

of the governing bodies were ever held there, and no
activities connected with them were either organized or
directed from there. On numerous occasions during my
stay at Liliesleaf farm I met both the Executive Committee
of the ANC, as well as the NHC, but such meetings were held
elsewhere and not on the farm.

(e) Whilst staying at Liliesleaf farm, I frequently visited
Arthur Goldreich in the main house and he also paid me
visits in my room. We had numerous political discussions
covering a variety of subjects. We discussed ideological and
practical questions, the Congress Alliance, Umkonto and
its activities generally, and his experiences as a soldier in
the Palmach, the military wing of the Haganah. Haganah
was the political authority of the Jewish National Movement
in Palestine.

(f) Because of what I had got to know of Goldreich, I recom-
mended on my return to South Africa that he should be
recruited to Umkonto. I do not know of my personal
knowledge whether this was done.

Another of the allegations made by the State is that the aims and
objects of the ANC and the Communist Party are the same. I wish
to deal with this and with my own political position, because I
must assume that the State may try to argue from certain Exhibits
that I tried to introduce Marxism into the ANC. The allegation as
to the ANC is false. This is an old allegation which was disproved at
the Treason Trial and which has again reared its head. But since
the allegation has been made again, I shall deal with it as well as
with the relationship between the ANC and the Communist Party
and Umkonto and that party.

The ideological creed of the ANC is, and always has been, the
creed of African Nationalism. It is not the concept of African
Nationalism expressed in the cry, 'Drive the White man into the
sea'. The African Nationalism for which the ANC stands is the
concept of freedom and fulfilment for the African people in their
own land. The most important political document ever adopted
by the ANC is the 'Freedom Charter'. It is by no means a blueprint
for a socialist state. It calls for redistribution, but not nationalization, of land; it provides for nationalization of mines, banks, and

monopoly industry, because big monopolies are owned by one race only, and without such nationalization racial domination would be perpetuated despite the spread of political power. It would be a hollow gesture to repeal the Gold Law prohibitions against Africans when all gold mines are owned by European companies. In this respect the ANC's policy corresponds with the old policy of the present Nationalist Party which, for many years, had as part of its programme the nationalization of the gold mines which, at that time, were controlled by foreign capital. Under the Freedom Charter, nationalization would take place in an economy based on private enterprise. The realization of the Freedom Charter would open up fresh fields for a prosperous African population of all classes, including the middle class. The ANC has never at any period of its history advocated a revolutionary change in the economic structure of the country, nor has it, to the best of my recollection, ever condemned capitalist society.

As far as the Communist Party is concerned, and if I understand its policy correctly, it stands for the establishment of a State based on the principles of Marxism. Although it is prepared to work for the Freedom Charter, as a short-term solution to the problems created by White supremacy, it regards the Freedom Charter as the beginning, and not the end, of its programme.

The ANC, unlike the Communist Party, admitted Africans only as members. Its chief goal was, and is, for the African people to win unity and full political rights. The Communist Party's main aim, on the other hand, was to remove the capitalists and to replace them with a working-class government. The Communist Party sought to emphasize class distinctions whilst the ANC seeks to harmonize them. This is a vital distinction.

It is true that there has often been close cooperation between the ANC and the Communist Party. But cooperation is merely proof of a common goal—in this case the removal of White supremacy—and is not proof of a complete community of interests.

The history of the world is full of similar examples. Perhaps the most striking illustration is to be found in the cooperation between Great Britain, the United States of America, and the Soviet Union in the fight against Hitler. Nobody but Hitler would have dared to suggest that such cooperation turned

Churchill or Roosevelt into communists or communist tools, or that Britain and America were working to bring about a communist world.

Another instance of such cooperation is to be found precisely in Umkonto. Shortly after Umkonto was constituted, I was informed by some of its members that the Communist Party would support Umkonto, and this then occurred. At a later stage the support was made openly.

I believe that communists have always played an active role in the fight by colonial countries for their freedom, because the short-term objects of communism would always correspond with the long-term objects of freedom movements. Thus communists have played an important role in the freedom struggles fought in countries such as Malaya, Algeria, and Indonesia, yet none of these States today are communist countries. Similarly in the underground resistance movements which sprung up in Europe during the last World War, communists played an important role. Even General Chiang Kai-Shek, today one of the bitterest enemies of communism, fought together with the communists against the ruling class in the struggle which led to his assumption of power in China in the 1930s.

This pattern of cooperation between communists and non-communists has been repeated in the National Liberation Movement of South Africa. Prior to the banning of the Communist Party, joint campaigns involving the Communist Party and the Congress movements were accepted practice. African communists could, and did, become members of the ANC, and some served on the National, Provincial, and local committees. Amongst those who served on the National Executive are Albert Nzula, a former Secretary of the Communist Party, Moses Kotane, another former Secretary, and J. B. Marks, a former member of the Central Committee.

I joined the ANC in 1944, and in my younger days I held the view that the policy of admitting communists to the ANC, and the close cooperation which existed at times on specific issues between the ANC and the Communist Party, would lead to a watering down of the concept of African Nationalism. At that stage I was a member of the African National Congress Youth League, and was one of a group which moved for the expulsion of communists from the ANC. This proposal was heavily defeated. Amongst those who voted against the proposal were some of the most conservative sections of African political opinion. They defended the policy on the ground that from its inception the ANC was formed and built up, not as a political party with one school of political thought, but as a Parliament of the African people, accommodating people of various political convictions, all united by the common goal of national liberation. I was eventually won over to this point of view and I have upheld it ever since.

It is perhaps difficult for White South Africans, with an ingrained prejudice against communism, to understand why experienced African politicians so readily accept communists as their friends. But to us the reason is obvious. Theoretical differences amongst those fighting against oppression is a luxury we cannot afford at this stage. What is more, for many decades communists were the only political group in South Africa who were prepared to treat Africans as human beings and their equals; who were prepared to eat with us; talk with us, live with us, and work with us. They were the only political group which was prepared to work with the Africans for the attainment of political rights and a stake in society. Because of this, there are many Africans who, today, tend to equate freedom with communism. They are supported in this belief by a legislature which brands all exponents of democratic government and African freedom as communists and bans many of them (who are communists) under the Suppression of Communism Act. Although I have never been a member of the Communist Party, I myself have been named under that pernicious Act because of the role I played in the Defiance Campaign. I have also been banned and imprisoned under that Act.

It is not only in internal politics that we count communists as amongst those who support our cause. In the international field, communist countries have always come to our aid. In the United Nations and other Councils of the world the communist *bloc* has supported the Afro-Asian struggle against colonialism and often seems to be more sympathetic to our plight than some of the Western powers. Although there is a universal condemnation of apartheid, the communist *bloc* speaks out against it with a louder voice than most of the White world. In these circumstances, it would take a brash young politician, such as I was in 1949, to proclaim that the Communists are our enemies.

I turn now to my own position. I have denied that I am a communist, and I think that in the circumstances I am obliged to state exactly what my political beliefs are.

I have always regarded myself, in the first place, as an African patriot. After all, I was born in Umtata, forty-six years ago. My guardian was my cousin, who was the acting paramount chief of Tembuland, and I am related both to the present paramount chief of Tembuland, Sabata Dalinyebo, and to Kaizer Matanzima, the Chief Minister of the Transkei.

Today I am attracted by the idea of a classless society, an attraction which springs in part from Marxist reading and, in part, from my admiration of the structure and organization of early African societies in this country. The land, then the main means of production, belonged to the tribe. There were no rich or poor and there was no exploitation.

It is true, as I have already stated, that I have been influenced by Marxist thought. But this is also true of many of the leaders of the new independent States. Such widely different persons as Gandhi, Nehru, Nkrumah, and Nasser all acknowledge this fact. We all accept the need for some form of socialism to enable our people to catch up with the advanced countries of this world and to overcome their legacy of extreme poverty. But this does not mean we are Marxists.

Indeed, for my own part, I believe that it is open to debate whether the Communist Party has any specific role to play at this particular stage of our political struggle. The basic task at the present moment is the removal of race discrimination and the attainment of democratic rights on the basis of the Freedom Charter. In so far as that Party furthers this task, I welcome its assistance. I realize that it is one of the means by which people of all races can be drawn into our struggle.

From my reading of Marxist literature and from conversations with Marxists, I have gained the impression that communists regard the parliamentary system of the West as undemocratic and reactionary. But, on the contrary, I am an admirer of such a system.

The Magna Carta, the Petition of Rights, and the Bill of Rights are documents which are held in veneration by democrats throughout the world.

I have great respect for British political institutions, and for the country's system of justice. I regard the British Parliament as the most democratic institution in the world, and the independence and impartiality of its judiciary never fail to arouse my admiration.

The American Congress, that country's doctrine of separation of powers, as well as the independence of its judiciary, arouses in me similar sentiments.

I have been influenced in my thinking by both West and East. All this has led me to feel that in my search for a political formula, I should be absolutely impartial and objective. I should tie myself to no particular system of society other than of socialism. I must leave myself free to borrow the best from the West and from the East.

There are certain Exhibits which suggest that we received financial support from abroad, and I wish to deal with this question.

Our political struggle has always been financed from internal sources—from funds raised by our own people and by our own supporters. Whenever we had a special campaign or an important political case—for example, the Treason Trial—we received financial assistance from sympathetic individuals and organizations in the Western countries. We had never felt it necessary to go beyond these sources.

But when in 1961 the Umkonto was formed, and a new phase of struggle introduced, we realized that these events would make a heavy call on our slender resources, and that the scale of our activities would be hampered by the lack of funds. One of my instructions, as I went abroad in January 1962, was to raise funds from the African states.

I must add that, whilst abroad, I had discussions with leaders of political movements in Africa and discovered that almost every single one of them, in areas which had still not attained independence, had received all forms of assistance from the socialist countries, as well as from the West, including that of financial support. I also discovered that some well-known African states, all of them non-communists, and even anti-communists, had received similar assistance.

On my return to the Republic, I made a strong recommendation to the ANC that we should not confine ourselves to Africa and the Western countries, but that we should also send a mission to the socialist countries to raise the funds which we so urgently needed.

I have been told that after I was convicted such a mission was sent, but I am not prepared to name any countries to which it went, nor am I at liberty to disclose the names of the organizations and countries which gave us support or promised to do so.

As I understand the State case, and in particular the evidence of 'Mr X', the suggestion is that Umkonto was the inspiration of the Communist Party which sought by playing upon imaginary grievances to enrol the African people into an army which ostensibly was to fight for African freedom, but in reality was fighting for a communist state. Nothing could be further from the truth. In fact the suggestion is preposterous. Umkonto was formed by Africans to further their struggle for freedom in their own land. Communists and others supported the movement, and we only wish that more sections of the community would join us.

Our fight is against real, and not imaginary, hardships or, to use the language of the State Prosecutor, 'so-called hardships'. Basically, we fight against two features which are the hallmarks of African life in South Africa and which are entrenched by legislation which we seek to have repealed. These features are poverty and lack of human dignity, and we do not need communists or so-called 'agitators' to teach us about these things.

South Africa is the richest country in Africa, and could be one of the richest countries in the world. But it is a land of extremes and remarkable contrasts. The Whites enjoy what may well be the highest standard of living in the world, whilst Africans live in poverty and misery. Forty per cent of the Africans live in hopelessly overcrowded and, in some cases, drought-stricken Reserves, where soil erosion and the overworking of the soil makes it impossible for them to live properly off the land. Thirty per cent are labourers, labour tenants, and squatters on White farms and work and live under conditions similar to those of the serfs of the Middle Ages. The other 30 per cent live in towns where they have developed economic and social habits which bring them closer in many respects to White standards. Yet most Africans, even in this group, are impoverished by low incomes and high cost of living.

The highest-paid and the most prosperous section of urban African life is in Johannesburg. Yet their actual position is desperate. The latest figures were given on 25 March 1964 by Mr Carr, Manager of the Johannesburg Non-European Affairs Department. The poverty datum line for the average African family in Johannesburg (according to Mr Carr's department) is R42·84 per month. He showed that the average monthly wage is R32·24 and that 46 per cent of all African families in Johannesburg do not earn enough to keep them going.

Poverty goes hand in hand with malnutrition and disease. The incidence of malnutrition and deficiency diseases is very high amongst Africans. Tuberculosis, pellagra, kwashiorkor, gastro-enteritis, and scurvy bring death and destruction of health. The incidence of infant mortality is one of the highest in the world. According to the Medical Officer of Health for Pretoria, tuberculosis kills forty people a day (almost all Africans), and in 1961 there were 58,491 new cases reported. These diseases not only destroy the vital organs of the body, but they result in retarded mental conditions and lack of initiative, and reduce powers of concentration. The secondary results of such conditions affect the whole community and the standard of work performed by African labourers.

The complaint of Africans, however, is not only that they are poor and the Whites are rich, but that the laws which are made by the Whites are designed to preserve this situation. There are two ways to break out of poverty. The first is by formal education, and the second is by the worker acquiring a greater skill at his work and thus higher wages. As far as Africans are concerned, both these avenues of advancement are deliberately curtailed by legislation.

The present Government has always sought to hamper Africans in their search for education. One of their early acts, after coming into power, was to stop subsidies for African school feeding. Many African children who attended schools depended on this supplement to their diet. This was a cruel act.

There is compulsory education for all White children at virtually no cost to their parents, be they rich or poor. Similar facilities are not provided for the African children, though there are some who receive such assistance. African children, however, generally have to pay more for their schooling than Whites. According to figures quoted by the South African Institute of Race Relations in its 1963 journal, approximately 40 per cent of African children in the age group between seven to fourteen do not attend school. For those who do attend school, the standards are vastly different from those afforded to White children. In 1960–61 the *per capita* Government spending on African students at State-aided schools was estimated at R12·46. In the same years, the *per capita* spending on White children in the Cape Province (which are the only figures available to me) was R144·57. Although there are no figures available to me, it can be stated, without doubt, that the White children on whom R144·57 per head was being spent all came from wealthier homes than African children on whom R12·46 per head was being spent.

The quality of education is also different. According to the Bantu Educational Journal, only 5,660 African children in the whole of South Africa passed their J.C. in 1962, and in that year only 362 passed matric. This is presumably consistent with the policy of Bantu education about which the present Prime Minister said, during the debate on the Bantu Education Bill in 1953:

'When I have control of Native education I will reform it so that Natives will be taught from childhood to realize that equality with Europeans is not for them . . . People who believe in equality are not desirable teachers for Natives. When my Department controls Native education it will know for what class of higher education a Native is fitted, and whether he will have a chance in life to use his knowledge.'

The other main obstacle to the economic advancement of the African is the industrial colour-bar under which all the better jobs of industry are reserved for Whites only. Moreover, Africans who do obtain employment in the unskilled and semi-skilled occupations which are open to them are not allowed to form trade unions which have recognition under the Industrial Conciliation Act. This means that strikes of African workers are illegal, and that they are denied the right of collective bargaining which is permitted to the better-paid White workers. The discrimination in the policy of successive South African Governments towards African workers is demonstrated by the so-called 'civilized labour policy' under which sheltered, unskilled Government jobs are found for those White workers who cannot make the grade in industry, at wages which far exceeded the earnings of the average African employee in industry.

The Government often answers its critics by saying that Africans in South Africa are economically better off than the inhabitants of the other countries in Africa. I do not know whether this statement is true and doubt whether any comparison can be made without having regard to the cost-of-living index in such countries. But even if it is true, as far as the African people are concerned it is irrelevant. Our complaint is not that we are poor by comparison with people in other countries, but that we are poor by comparison with the White people in our own country, and that we are prevented by legislation from altering this imbalance.

The lack of human dignity experienced by Africans is the direct result of the policy of White supremacy. White supremacy implies Black inferiority. Legislation designed to preserve White supremacy entrenches this notion. Menial tasks in South Africa are invariably performed by Africans. When anything has to be carried or cleaned the White man will look around for an African to do it for him, whether the African is employed by him or not. Because of this sort of attitude, Whites tend to regard Africans as a separate breed. They do not look upon them as people with families of their own; they do not realize that they have emotions —that they fall in love like White people do; that they want to be with their wives and children like White people want to be with theirs; that they want to earn enough money to support their families properly, to feed and clothe them and send them to school. And what 'house-boy' or 'garden-boy' or labourer can ever hope to do this?

Pass laws, which to the Africans are among the most hated bits of legislation in South Africa, render any African liable to police surveillance at any time. I doubt whether there is a single African male in South Africa who has not at some stage had a brush with the police over his pass. Hundreds and thousands of Africans are thrown into jail each year under pass laws. Even worse than this is the fact that pass laws keep husband and wife apart and lead to the breakdown of family life.

Poverty and the breakdown of family life have secondary effects. Children wander about the streets of the townships because they have no schools to go to, or no money to enable them to go to school, or no parents at home to see that they go to school, because both parents (if there be two) have to work to keep the family alive. This leads to a breakdown in moral standards, to an alarming rise in illegitimacy, and to growing violence which erupts, not only politically, but everywhere. Life in the townships is dangerous. There is not a day that goes by without somebody being stabbed or assaulted. And violence is carried out of the townships in the White living areas. People are afraid to walk alone in the streets after dark. Housebreakings and robberies are increasing, despite the fact that the death sentence can now be imposed for such offences. Death sentences cannot cure the festering sore.

Africans want to be paid a living wage. Africans want to perform work which they are capable of doing, and not work which the Government declares them to be capable of. Africans want to be allowed to live where they obtain work, and not be endorsed out of an area because they were not born there. Africans want to be allowed to own land in places where they work, and not to be obliged to live in rented houses which they can never call their own. Africans want to be part of the general population, and not confined to living in their own ghettoes. African men want to have their wives and children to live with them where they work, and not be forced into an unnatural existence in men's hostels. African women want to be with their menfolk and not be left permanently widowed in the Reserves. Africans want to be allowed out after eleven o'clock at night and not to be confined to their rooms like little children. Africans want to be allowed to travel in their own country and to seek work where they want to and not where the Labour Bureau tells them to. Africans want a just share in the whole of South Africa; they want security and a stake in society.

Above all, we want equal political rights, because without them our disabilities will be permanent. I know this sounds revolutionary to the Whites in this country, because the majority of voters will be Africans. This makes the White man fear democracy.

But this fear cannot be allowed to stand in the way of the only solution which will guarantee racial harmony and freedom for all. It is not true that the enfranchisement of all will result in racial domination. Political division, based on colour, is entirely artificial and, when it disappears, so will the domination of one colour group by another. The ANC has spent half a century fighting against racialism. When it triumphs it will not change that policy.

This then is what the ANC is fighting. Their struggle is a truly national one. It is a struggle of the African people, inspired by their own suffering and their own experience. It is a struggle for the right to live.

During my lifetime I have dedicated myself to this struggle of the African people. I have fought against White domination, and I have fought against Black domination. I have cherished the ideal of a democratic and free society in which all persons live together in harmony and with equal opportunities. It is an ideal which I hope to live for and to achieve. But if needs be, it is an ideal for which I am prepared to die.

THE Rivonia trial ended eleven months and a day after the police swoop on the underground headquarters. Of the nine men in the dock, one, 'Rusty' Bernstein, was found not guilty and acquitted. Mandela, Sisulu, Mbeki, Mhlaba, Motsoaledi, Mlangeni, Kathrada, and Goldberg—six Africans, an Indian, and a White—were sentenced to life imprisonment.

They stood erect to hear the sentence and when it was passed they turned in a body to the packed Court, smiled, and waved their arms. They were led from the dock to the cells below. Outside the courtroom a sector of the crowd burst into song when the sentence became known and unfurled banners, one of which read: 'You will not serve these sentences as long as we live.' As he was driven away under heavy guard, Mandela gave the thumbs-up 'Afrika!' salute of the African National Congress.

The night following the passing of sentence he was flown to Cape Town and taken by ferry to Robben Island, the maximum-security penal island used for South African political prisoners.

A Selected List of Non-Fiction Available from Mandarin

While every effort is made to keep prices low, it is sometimes necessary to increase prices at short notice. Mandarin Paperbacks reserves the right to show new retail prices on covers which may differ from those previously advertised in the text or elsewhere.

The prices shown below were correct at the time of going to press.

All these books are available at your bookshop or newsagent, or can be ordered direct from the publisher. Just tick the titles you want and fill in the form below.

Mandarin Paperbacks, Cash Sales Department, PO Box 11, Falmouth, Cornwall TR10 9EN.

Please send cheque or postal order, no currency, for purchase price quoted and allow the following for postage and packing:

UK	80p for the first book, 20p for each additional book ordered to a maximum charge of £2.00.
BFPO	80p for the first book, 20p for each additional book.
Overseas including Eire	£1.50 for the first book, £1.00 for the second and 30p for each additional book thereafter.

NAME (Block letters) ....

ADDRESS ....

....

....